TRANSLATORS AND TRANSLATIONS

GREEK - DANISH

edited by

Henrik Holmboe and Signe Isager

THE DANISH INSTITUTE AT ATHENS
2001

Copyright: The Danish Institute at Athens, 2001
Printed in Greece
by Graphic Arts Leonidas G. Karydakis, Athens

ISBN 87 7934 003 2

Distributed by:
AARHUS UNIVERSITY PRESS
Langelandsgade 177
DK-8200 Aarhus N
Fax: (0045) 8942 5380

73 Lime Walk
Headington
Oxford OX3 7AD
Fax (0044) 01865 750 079

100 Main St.
Box 511
Oakville, Connecticut 06779
Fax (001) 860 945 9468

Cover: Nina Hole
1998

Contents

Preface ... 7

Otto Steen Due:
    The Forging of a New Danish Iliad. ... 9

Jørgen Mejer:
    Translating Greek Tragedy. The Text on the Page,
    The Drama on the Stage. ... 15

Minna Skafte Jensen:
    How Ancient Greek Literature Reached Danish Readers. ... 25

Lene Andersen:
    Translating the Bible. ... 35

Chr. Gorm Tortzen:
    Translations and Classical Civilization in
    the Danish Gymnasium. ... 45

Takis Kayalis:
    European Literature in Translation: Research at the
    Center for the Greek Language. ... 53

Rolf Hesse:
    Modern Greek Literature in Danish Translation. ... 59

Note on Bibliography ... 63

Sophia Scopetea:
    On Translating S. Kierkegaard's *Philosophical
    Fragments* into Greek. ... 65

Lars Nørgaard:
    Achilleus Paraschos and Two Danish Folk Songs.   73

Aristea Papanicolaou-Christensen:
    Translating into Greek from Danish 19th Century Texts   115

Dimitris Papanikolaou:
    How Danish and Greek Legal Languages Meet in the
    Multilingual Environment of the European Community.   119

Leo Kalovyrnas:
    Eurospeak: Neologisms and Other Translatory Phenomena
    in Danish and Greek. The European Parliament Minutes
    and Reports Corpus.   129

Niels Jæger:
    Translation from Modern Greek into Danish at the
    EU institutions.   143

Henrik Gottlieb:
    Texts, Translation and Subtitling – in Theory,
    and in Denmark.   149

Iannis Papadakis:
    Subtitling in Greece.
    The Fear of the Goalie at the Penalty Kick   193

Frieda Charalabopoulou:
    Short Description of the CD-ROM "Filoglossia"   201

List of Contributors   203

> "The affair at Babel confirmed and externalized
> the never-ending task of the translator -
> it did not initiate it."
> George Steiner

Preface

The art of translation is vital in a literal as well as a figurative sense of the word and has been so since time immemorial. A heavy responsibility rests on the translator. The problems inherent in producing a loyal translation are innumerable. They vary according to the character of the text and to the chosen or given target of the translation, - and yet there are general problems. These are met in all their variety in countries like Denmark and Greece, since neither Greek nor Danish is a world language. Therefore, while discussing the general problems presented by translating, this book has its focus on Denmark and Greece and on the following pairs of language:

Modern Greek - Danish
Danish - Modern Greek
Ancient Greek - Modern Greek
Ancient Greek - Danish

Or at least that was the plan: The observant reader will look in vain for a contribution on the translation of Ancient Greek into Modern Greek. Much to our regret we had to leave that important aspect out in the very last moment.

The present volume is a result of the seminar *Translators and Translations, Greek-Danish,* which took place at The Danish Institute at Athens, September 23 - 26, 1999. Another result is a bibliography of Modern Greek Literature translated into Danish and covering the period 1831-1998, prepared for and presented at the seminar. The seminar was arranged by Rolf Hesse, Henrik Holmboe and The Danish Institute and should be seen as a continuation of the fruitful collaboration between various institutions and professions in Denmark and in Greece created during the preparation of the two dictionaries by Rolf Hesse, Danish-Modern Greek (*Dansk-Nygræsk Ordbog*), Copenhagen 1995, and Modern Greek-Danish (*Ελληνοδανικό Λεξικό*), Athens 1998, 3rd edition 2000. All contributors to the book have Greek or Danish as their mother tongue. They are professionally engaged in translation and represent very different fields. The book does not pretend to be exhaustive nor to present final solutions. We hope it will be read for the information it contains and that it will form a basis for further discussion.

Warm thanks are due to the Royal Danish Ministry of Research and The Eleni Nakou Foundation for the financial support received both for the seminar and for the present publication.

The Danish Institute at Athens	Signe Isager
December 2000	Director

The Forging of a New Danish Iliad

by
Otto Steen Due

In European literature Homer begins to supplant Vergil as the undisputed king of poets in the early eighteenth century as part of the long *querelle des anciens et des modernes*, and the Homeric Question, a discussion of paramount importance for European culture, was founded with works such as Giambattista Vico's *Principii di scienza nuova* (1744), Thomas Blackwell's *An Enquiry into the Life and Writings of Homer* from 1735, translated in 1775 by J. H. Voss, Voss's own translations of the poems and F. A. Wolf's *Prolegomena* (1795) and many others within the arena now denoted by cultural historians as the Republic of Letters, including people like Jean Jacques Rousseau and Ludvig Holberg.

But one hundred years before, a contemporary of William Shakespeare, George Chapman, had produced translations of the Iliad (1611) and the Odyssey (1616), which became 'classics' of English literature. England was at the beginning of the Renascence a half-barbarous country. But during the Renascence she and her language absorbed, in that turbulent, voracious and uncouth manner which is characteristic of upstarts, French and Italian culture, appropriating, even stealing and rather superficially adapting their vocabulary, little concerned and inhibited by the more sophisticated standards of taste already established in continental Europe. In that process English acquired that unique character of *mixtum compositum*, which would, eventually, make it irresistible as a modern *koine*. English does not have the puristic inhibitions, which so heavily haunt French, for instance. English is still able to eat and digest virtually any other language's terms. The struggle between the ancients and the moderns thus became an issue in England with the delay of roughly a century. Alexander Pope's Homer (1713-26) for a time ensconced the poems within the confines of neoclassicism according to the taste of the moderns, but the epics would not long be so contained.

In Denmark, too, a number of experiments were made in the latter half of the eighteenth century, aiming at a Danish Homer, but no Danish Pope emerged before the Romantic Revolution against the rationalism of the preceding century had taken place around 1800 and outdated any such project. The poet, scholar and philosopher Poul Martin Möller produced between 1816 and 1825 seven songs of the Odyssey, and if he had continued, his Odyssey would have proved to become the standard Danish translation of that poem for generations.

In the twenties and the thirties a literary feud was fought in Denmark with some resemblance to the historical quarrel of ancients and moderns. Should literature be national and Nordic, spontaneously inspired, romantic, based on personal experience and feelings, eruptive in form, creative and ebullient, concrete, and founded on practice *or* should it be international and European, speculative and neoclassic, based on insight and intellect, regular and disciplined in form, descriptive and observant, and founded on poetical theory? The former position was taken by the 'ancients', rallied around the now ageing poet of romantic spring in our country, Adam Oehlenschläger, the latter was advocated by the emerging *arbiter* of taste, J. L. Heiberg, who aesthetically and poetically preferred French *esprit* to German *Geist*, paying full respect to the genius of the young Oehlenschläger, but considering his poetics primitive and obsolete in a modern context.

As a weighty contribution to and plea in this feud on the side of the 'ancients', a minor poet and a great translator, Christian Wilster, achieved for Danish literature what Chapman had done for English literature some two centuries before. Wilster's 'original' poetry is now forgotten. But his Homer (from 1836-37) has ever since remained the classical Danish Homer, giving many generations an experience which can best be illustrated by quoting John Keats' *On first looking into Chapman's Homer:*

> Much have I travelled in the realms of gold,
> and many goodly states and kingdoms seen;
> round many western islands have I been
> which bards in fealty to Apollo hold.
> Oft of one wide expanse had I been told
> that deep-browed Homer ruled as his demesne;

yet did I never breath its pure serene
till I heard Chapman speak out loud and bold;
Then felt I like some watcher of the skies
when a new planet swims into his ken;
or like stout Cortez, when with eagle eyes
he stared at the Pacific — and all his men
looked at each other with a wild surmise —
silent, upon a peak in Darien.

But more than thirty years of mistaken educational policy in Denmark and succesful combating of knowledge in school has now produced the result that pupils cannot any more read and understand literature written before 1870. It is now seriously envisaged, even by some educated people, to 'translate' or modernize older literature. In fact, this misfortune has already befallen some of Kierkegaard's works. Only one stronghold of historical literacy has not yet been destroyed. It is the reading of Wilster's Homer in the discipline 'Ancient culture' which is compulsory for all high-school students in their last year. But in the long run this discipline cannot bear the additional burden of doing what classes in Danish should have accomplished in eleven years. That is why a new translation has been sorely needed. To modernize indigenous literary masterpieces is certainly a questionable procedure. But nothing is more legitimate than the retranslation of foreign literature when old translations do not work effectively any more. Wilster will not in his heaven nurse any grudges against me for trying to replace him in Danish literature, not by modernizing his text, which has been tried with ridiculous results, but by an entirely new translation from Greek.

There are particularly two things which make Wilster difficult to enjoy for the general reader — and for most students. One is well illustrated by the poem of Keats I have just quoted. It was in English as it was in Danish poetry completely legitimate to deviate from natural and normal word order. Indeed, such inversions were both expected and appreciated in poetry. In Denmark this is not so any more. This poetic device is nowadays only found in songs produced by relatives or professional song writers to celebrate birthdays, silver weddings and the like. It has become what Germans call 'herabgesunkenes Kulturgut'. In serious modern poetry the effect of this poetic license is devastatingly ridiculous. So my entire Iliad does not contain any single inversion at all. To achieve that has not been an easy thing at all.

The other thing is the fact that stress since Wilster's days has shifted in a host of composite nouns and verbs. So he scans the word for 'gatherer of clouds', a most common epithet to Zeus, 'skys*a*mler' but the natural pronounciation nowadays is 'sk*y*samler' and the verb '*u*dlægge' meaning 'interpret (an omen)' will not scan, unless pronounced 'udl*æ*gge'; the adjective 'f*u*ldbyrdet' (accomplished) sounded in Wilster's days 'fuldb*y*rdet'. This development of Danish has the effect that every seventh line in his translations becomes unmetrical for modern readers who have no training in reading our classics, a training younger people do not possess any more. But they do have very well-trained ears for rhythm, and are quite able to hear when a line falters.

Another example: In Wilster's time there were two living words for 'not', viz. the elevated, slightly archaic and poetical 'ej' and the prosaic and colloquial 'ikke'. The advantage of metrically different equivalents for this extremely common word when you are writing modern dactylic hexameters, is obvious. Wilster nevertheless never ever uses 'ikke'. In the meantime 'ej' has disappeared in living Danish language except in songs of that subcultural character which I have just mentioned. It only survives in a very restricted number of fixed idioms. Apart from those I never ever use 'ej'.

Not surprisingly the concept or rather the content of *decorum* has changed considerably in the past five or six generations. When Achilles in book XXIII mentions the vows made by himself and his father to Spercheios before his departure for Troy, he also lists 'fifty uncastrated rams'. Here Wilster had some trouble, as the Danish word for 'testicles', viz. 'nosser', was under absolute taboo in his Biedermeier time. His solution is elegant enough but wasted on readers nowadays. Danish has a word for 'wether', i. e. 'castrated ram', viz. 'bede', still understood (approximately) thanks to a childrens' song still in use in kindergartens:

Ole sad på en knold og sang,
får og beder omkring ham sprang

(Ole sat on a knoll and sang,
sheep and wethers around him sprang).

Wilster's research at the Royal Library revealed an old verb 'bede', reported by the lexicographer Matthias Moth some 150 years before his time in an unpublished manuscript, meaning exactly 'to castrate rams'. So he constructed a participle with the privative prefix 'u-' (identical with English 'un-'): 'ub*e*dede' (with the stress of his time). This is not only incomprehensible to modern readers but bound to be misunderstood, as the only current meanings of the verb 'bede' — a homonym to the rural rarity unearthed by Wilster — is: 'to pray, ask or invite'. My own solution is 'benossede' a neologism, that's true, but understandable to anybody on first sight. It renders the Greek μῆλα ἔνορχα with perfect precision, meaning 'provided with balls'. But until 40 years ago 'nosser' ('balls') was a word so vulgar that children were slapped for using it. Now, it has almost entirely lost its vulgarity, as I believe is the case with 'balls' too, if not in English, at least in American.

So there are good reasons for making a new Danish Homer. These reasons are not, however my motive for doing it. The work is not owed to philological duty but — to be somewhat pompous — to artistic vocation.

The fate of my previous translations, the *Metamorphoses* of Ovid in 1989 and the *Aeneid* of Vergil in 1996 and the feed-back I have got from collegues, poets, critics, fellow-translators, students and children during the three years I have been working on the text permit me to be confident that my translation will effectively replace that of Wilster for at least thirty or forty years to come. It is unlikely that I shall live to know, and it is certain that I will not live to know whether my work shall prove as durable as Wilster's masterpieces.

I might add, as a kind of appendix to these short considerations, some remarks about poetical translation and its necessary method as I have experienced it in more than 15 years of intensive practice. I would, however, premise a remark to the effect that I am not much given to theoretical speculation on the subject and have a limited knowledge of the relevant learned literature which I find not very helpful for practioners and in most cases misleading and badly written.

The real problem is not to acquire a thorough mastery of the source language, including the source culture, contemporary or ancient as the case may be. That can be achieved by any (intelligent) person through hard work, application and tenacity. Nor is the problem to obtain full control of the target language, typically one's own mother language. Any (talented) person can do that by the same means. The real problem, as I see it, is to overcome the fact that the human brain is not designed to operate two languages simultaneously. I have been told by people who profess to know about it that physical damage of the brain may sometimes produce loss of either the mother language or a foreign language — or, of course, of both. It is a well-known fact that genuinely bilingual people never speek macaronic: they may shift from the one language to the other from period to period, or even in the middle of a period. But at any given moment they are speaking one language respecting its rules, including the rules of making blunders in it. The translator's crucial problem is to forget the source language's formulation completely, at the same time retaining it as a kind of linguistic plasma, a not yet verbally formulated need to be expressed in his (own) target language. To achieve this necessitates an extensive use of that most important part of our selves which is not confined to the narrow range of our consciousness. Too much concentration is often counterproductive. Sometimes it helps to attend to your garden or to take a walk. Sometimes a difficulty takes a good sleep to solve itself. Sometimes it takes a year. But — at least in my own case — the extended self proves unhelpful if the hard conscious homework has not been done properly.

Translating Greek Tragedy
The Text on the Page, The Drama on the Stage

by
Jørgen Mejer

Even the most literal translation is an interpretation: there are no two languages whose vocabularies correspond completely. To translate does not mean to transfer words from one language to another, that is impossible; translation means to transfer thoughts and feelings from one language and culture to another language and culture; translation takes place between two different cultures expressed in a linguistic form, not only between two different languages, like Greek and Danish, but also between two different stages of the same language, like ancient Greek into modern Greek; some people in Denmark are able to understand the best of all Danish dramatists, Ludvig Holberg, despite the fact that he wrote his comedies more than 250 years ago, in part because his plays have been performed continuously since their first appearance on the stage until today; but most Danes need a commentary to understand much of his vocabulary and syntax; the Norwegians who like to claim Holberg as a national author, cannot at all understand him, but must translate him into modern Norwegian.

Ancient dramas have not been kept alive by being put on the stage continuously since they were written 2500 years ago. The ancient dramatic tradition was broken off completely sometime in the late antiquity, indeed we know very little about how the ancient Greek plays were performed and acted, e. g. we know that music was important, but we have no idea how it sounded. All we have are words on the page, words that have been transmitted in manuscripts which do not always have identical texts, words which often have very obscure meanings (indeed some 10 % of the tragic vocabulary are hapax legomena), words whose connotations and allusive power often escape us. Indeed, there is no way to translate a Greek tragedy without taking responsibility for a particular interpretation of that play.

But the main difference between Greek dramatic texts and other literary texts is that plays in principle and principally are meant to be presented on a stage. The audience watching a performance is supposed to watch a drama being acted out, they are not supposed to think that this is a Greek tragedy as much as that it is a drama taking place before their eyes, they must be absorbed by the unfolding drama, its tensions and its resolutions of these tensions when this happens. This will only be the case when the dramatic text is comprehensible for the audience line by line, when the audience is not bothered with understanding the vocabulary as such because it is odd, quaint or old-fashioned - except when it is like that. When strange words do occur, the translation must, like the original, make the audience listen to catch the meanings of words that they cannot immediately understand.

Of course, a translation ought not to make the text easier than it is from the hand of the author, but the translator must carefully consider how the dramatic translation can remain dramatic when presented on the stage, i.e. which elements in the original text are necessary to preserve the drama, its ideas and emotions. The tragedy on the stage is to be enjoyed without previous study of the text, commentary, or introduction. The audience may very well experience a world that is different from their daily routine, but they should not constantly be reminded of a foreign language or style that they don't know. The expert may read or listen to the text thinking about the original, but the audience must experience the text as a play worth the price of the ticket. It is very possible that there must be a significant difference between translations meant to be studied by the Greekless reader in a school and a translation meant to be experienced by a member of the audience in a theater. In the school system we read translations in order to teach about Greek tragedy and culture and therefore must point out special features of the Greek original by means of commentary; in the theater the problem of the relationship between the Greek original and the translation ought to be felt by neither audience nor actors. In a good dramatic translation this problem has been solved by the translator: the text as performed must speak *directly* to the audience.

I am not sure that there are problems in translating ancient Greek tragedies into Danish that are different from translating these plays into any modern language - except that we have fewer dramatic models, or classics, in Denmark: the British have Shakespeare, the French Corneille and Racine, the Germans Schiller and Goethe: these authors have been performed continuously since they wrote, and they constitute a certain dramatic tradition in terms of vocabulary, style (including meters) and dramatic convention. Apart from Holberg we have nothing similar in Denmark. Shortly after 1800 Adam Oehlenschlaeger wrote a number of tragedies, in fact partly to recreate ancient Greek tragedy in a contemporary Danish style, and they were for more than 100 years very popular on the stage and in the schools; but he has not been popular in the XX century. Given the conservative nature of many philologists and their academic background, Danish translations of Greek tragedies until a generation ago imitated the style of Oehlenschlaeger, quite effectively provided that the audience knows the Danish dramatist. Since this is no longer the case, modern translations of Greek tragedy must find other ways of transferring the ancient dramas to a Danish audience. In the two modern productions of Greek tragedy at the Royal Theater in Copenhagen in the 90s, Sophocles' *King Oedipus* and Euripides' *Phoenician Women,* I have worked with one well-known Danish poet, Søren Ulrik Thomsen, who knows no Greek, but who has a fine sense of poetry and a great ability to create poetic expressions in the Danish language. We were determined to present these tragedies in a way that would give the audience a sense of the drama and an impression of the poetry of the tragedies: we used modern poetic language and we avoided use of old-fashioned vocabulary because we felt that we would betray the original texts if the text of the plays did not speak directly to an audience that knew no Greek, but had a desire to listen to a poetic, dramatic text which dealt with basic problems and basic feelings in human life. We knew that the audience was unprepared for the ancient tragedies, and we made it our duty to make sure that they would experience the dramas just by being present in the auditorium and being drawn in by the words and the action on the stage.

All translators translate for a particular audience, i.e. the translation is not only limited by the translator's understanding of the source language and his ability to express himself in the target language, but also by the audience for whom he is translating. Though it is difficult to forget one's colleagues who often will be the closest to evaluate the product, it is important to be aware that many features of ancient dramatic texts which had significance for the audience in antiquity can impede the modern audience's understanding and enjoyment. One, perhaps extreme example of this can be found in Ezra Pound's version of Sophocles' *Trachiniae* lines 517-525 [see table 1]

Sophocles Trachiniae 517-525

τότ' ἦν χερός, ἦν δὲ τόξων πάταγος ταυρείων τ' ἀνάμιγδα κεράτων, ἦν δ' ἀμφίπλεκτοι κλίμακες, ἦν δὲ μετώπων ὀλόεντα πλήγματα καὶ στόνος ἀμφοῖν. ἁ δ' εὐῶπις ἁβρὰ τηλαυγεῖ παρ' ὄχθῳ ἧστο, τὸν ὃν προσμένουσ' ἀκοίταν.	Then there was thudding of fists and clang of bows and confusion of bulls' horns; and there was contorted grappling and there were deadly blows from butting heads and groaning on both sides. But the tender girl with the lovely eyes sat far from them on a hillside, waiting for the one who would be her husband.	ROCK and wrack, Horns into back, Slug, grunt and groan, Grip through to bone. Crash and thud Bows against blood Grip and grind Bull's head and horn. BUT the wide-eyed girl on the hill, Out of it all, frail, Who shall have her?
	Michael Jameson 1957	Ezra Pound 1956

Easterling on 517-30: The duel itself was a confusion of violence and noise, and the girl who was to be the battle prize sat apart in terror. On 517-22: the use of anaphora and of the figure which the ancient critics called *schema Pindaricum*... contributes to the elevated effect... the main emphasis is on the noise made by all these together...
On 523-5: τηλαυγεῖ The emphasis here seems to be on Deianeira's remoteness from the scene of the duel, rather than on her ability to watch it.
Long (*Language and Thought in Sophocles* p. 76): the fight is expressed impersonally, as a series of short alternate actions... Each stage of the contest is described by verbal nouns limited by an adj. and defining genitive. The use of nouns instead of verbs has an abrupt effect which harmonizes admirably with the events described.

If you study the modern commentaries you will find that Pound has managed to express what goes on in the text quite well.

Another problem which may impede the understanding of the modern audience is that the Greek gods mean little nowadays but that they play an integral role in tragedy. The name 'Apollo' may mean a lot to you and me, and meant even more for the ancient audience whether Apollo was called Φοῖβος, Φοῖβος ἑκαβόλος, Λύκειος, Λοξίας, all terms which are used in Sophocles' *King Oedipus*; but if you try to use all these expressions on the stage to denote one and the same god, the audience will be confused. It is not that it is insignificant which expressions are being used: Φοῖβος is used by Oedipus himself in particular and indicates his reverend attitude towards the god, Λύκειος is used twice in the context of prayer, Λοξίας is used when speaking about Apollo as an oracular god. The one time when Oedipus uses simply 'Apollo', is when he accuses the god of being responsible for his misdeeds, and when Iocasta does the same, also only once, it is when she accuses the god of making a false prediction. But on the modern stage, the translator better settle on one name and then attempt to express the connotations which the various names carry, in other ways.

As a general rule, the numerous names in Greek drama should be rendered with great sensibility. It is far too easy just to transcribe the name, e.g. a geographical name, without determining why it is being used. Two examples from Euripides' *Phoenician Women* may illustrate this problem:

In the beginning of the play Antigone asks the old servant to identify some of the leaders of the enemy; when he points at yet another general, Antigone asks (lines 133-35):

ἄλλος ἄλλος ὅδε τευχέων τρόπος.
τίς δ᾽ ἐστιν οὗτος; Πα. παῖς μὲν Οἰνέως ἔφυ
Τυδεύς, Ἄρη δ᾽ Αἰτωλὸν ἐν στέρνοις ἔχει.

How strange, how strange his arms! And who is he?
Tydeus, son of Oeneus, he has Aetolian courage (Ares) in his breast.

Apart from the fact that it is necessary to turn the warrior god Ares into an abstract noun in a translation, the name Aetolian does not tell the modern reader or spectator anything. The ancient Greek audience knew that warriors from Aetolia were considered tough and eager to fight (so even in Thucydides); so what we have to express in our translation is that this is a warrior of extraordinary qualities. It may be important in a study of ancient Greek psychology to notice that courage is located in the breast but this is not important in the dramatic context. Hence we translated in our version:

(An): Hvem er han? Hans rustning ser ud på en helt, helt anden måde
(Tj): Hans navn er Tydeus, og han er kendt som en rasende kriger.

A little further on in the play the chorus expresses fear of the Argive army (lines 256-7):

Ἄργος ὦ Πελασγικόν,
δειμαίνω τὰν σὰν ἀλκὰν
καὶ τὸ θεόθεν

The standard translation calls Argos 'Pelasgian' and does not indicate why this adjective is used here; the point is surely that Argos and Pelasgos for the ancient Greeks represented the oldest layer of Greek civilization and was considered with respect. We try to express this by translating:

Bomstærke Argos, berygtede stormagt,
jeg skælver for din og for himmelens hånd.

In some cases the intervention may be more extensive - and questionable. At the end of the central stasimon in *King Oedipus*, the chorus is concerned with the fate of religion:

King Oedipus lines 897-902:
οὐκέτι τὸν ἄθικτον εἶμι
    γᾶς ἐπ' ὀμφαλὸν σέβων,
οὐδ' ἐς τὸν Ἀβαῖσι ναόν,
    οὐδὲ τὰν Ὀλυμπίαν,
εἰ μὴ τάδε χειδόδεικτα
    πᾶσιν ἁρμόσαι βροτοῖς.

I shall no longer go to the untouchable
navel of the earth worshipping,
nor to the temple in Abae
nor to Olympia,
unless these oracles do come right
and be pointed at by all human beings.

The last clause is quite obscure, in the sense that the verb is hard to translate and the adjective is an hapax legomenon. On the other hand, it is evident that the meaning is that the oracles given to Oedipus must be assumed to be true and to be obvious to all. The first part of the statement is clear to the expert: there was an oracle dedicated to Apollo in Abae and prophecy was made from the ashes at the Zeus altar in Olympia. But to a modern audience these names make no sense: Abae is unknown and Olympia is associated with the Olympian games. Consequently, one must interpret to translate:

Hvis denne profeti ikke bli'r til virkelighed
for øjnene af hele verden,
så rejser jeg aldrig mere til Delfi, Jordens hellige navle,
eller til noget andet orakel.

I would claim that this adequately represents the meaning of the Greek text, even though the word σέβων has been skipped; but this participle is implicit in the sense that no one would take the trouble to travel to an oracle unless it was part of worshipping the god. By leaving out the two geographical names we can make the request of the chorus evident, by adding Delphi we avoid confusing the audience with yet another name for Delphi, and by reversing the order of the clauses, the issue becomes as clear-cut as it is in the Greek text. And compared to other Danish translations this version is much more true to the Greek text.

Sometimes it is necessary to unfold the rather compressed mythical passages in the Greek original so that an audience can comprehend the text as a story in itself. This 'help to the reader/listener' may be questionable, but it is, I believe, important to maintain the dramatic tension.

The episode in the *Phoenician Women* (lines 834-1018) with Creon, Teiresias and Menoeceus is rich in mythological allusions and references, in particular in the passage where Teiresias explains why it is up to Creon to save Thebes by sacrificing his own son (lines 930-40):

ὀρθῶς μ' ἐρωτᾷς κεἰς ἀγῶν' ἔρχῃ λόγων.
δεῖ τόνδε θαλάμαις, οὗ δράκων ὁ γηγενὴς
ἐγένετο Δίρκης ναμάτων ἐπίσκοπος,
σφαγέντα φόνιον αἷμα γῇ δοῦναι χοάς

Κάδμου παλαιῶν Ἄρεος ἐκ μηνιμάτων,
ὃς γηγενεῖ δράκοντι τιμωρεῖ φόνον.
καὶ ταῦτα δρῶντες σύμμαχον κτήσεσθ' Ἄρη.
χθὼν δ' ἀντὶ καρποῦ καρπὸν ἀντὶ θ' αἵματος
αἷμ' ἢν λάβῃ βρότειον, ἕξετ' εὐμενῆ
γῆν, ἥ ποθ' ὑμῖν χρυσοπήληκα στάχυν
Σπαρτῶν ἀνῆκεν.

In some ways this mythological account is meant to refer to something remote and possibly irrelevant, but it is very difficult to make an audience understand what is going on except by an extensive commentary - which you cannot get across to the audience during a performance. Hence it is necessary to tell the myth in a way which makes sense to the audience, by offering a few extra pieces of information and by rearranging the elements of the story. At the beginning of the passage we have tried to create an atmosphere of the folk tale. At the end of lines 930-40 it would confuse the audience to bring in the Theban Spartoí (which all would assume were men from Sparta) or to give the etymological meaning of the word: "the golden-helmeted crop [ears of corn] of the sown men" (as the old Danish translation does). Now, both the mention of the Spartoi and the imagery are very striking, and the question the translator must ask is why Euripides uses them here. We have interpreted them to mean that Euripides wants to stress a fact that belongs to the good old days of the Theban people; we have sacrificed the golden helmets and substituted spears, which give the impression of the mass of men springing forth from the earth. Our translation is true to the meaning of the original text even if we chose to express it in a slightly different way:

> Du er i din gode ret til at kræve et svar, og det skal du få.
> Den drage, som Ares lod føde af jorden
> for at dén skulle vogte floden, den sorte,
> der slynger sig gennem vort vidtstrakte land,
> blev dræbt af Kong Kadmos, så Ares bærer
> den dag i dag på et brændende nag,
> og han kræver at se en søn af din slægt
> ofret så blodet simpelthen siler
> ned i den jord, der var mor til hans drage.

Gi'r du et barn for et barn vil Ares
stå skulder til skulder med dig i krigen,
og ofrer du blod for blod, kan du vinde
en forbundsfælle i selveste jorden,
der i sin tid lod jeres slægt skyde op
som hvedens titusinde glinsende spyd.

The rhythm of the Danish translation in the last example brings us to another major problem when translating ancient drama: how to render the meters of ancient drama in a modern translation? It has long been tradition to find some approximation to the iambic trimeters, the most commonly used meter in non-lyrical passages; often blank verse because this meter was used in European drama for a long time, but whatever the approximation, the modern rhythm has been based on stress, not the interplay of long and short syllables. The choral lyrics have been turned into various metrical strophes usually not similar to the ancient Greek, though often the ancient structure of strophe, anti-strophe and epode has been preserved. Much bad poetry has been the result, and the similarity is at best dubious. The important thing is, it seems to me, that the translation presents poetic images and expressions of feelings and thoughts which correspond to the original text.

The choral lyrics were written and performed in metrical structures which we unfortunately are unable to associate with any particular meaning. For that reason - and because no modern chorus will perform in a way that corresponds to the ancient chorus -, it makes no sense to try to imitate the formalities of ancient dramatic lyrics.

But what about the iambic trimeters? The modern Danish audience does not associate anything with blank verse, and blank verse in Danish translations in general means unnatural reversed word order and various pseudo-archaic vocabulary which have no justification from the point of view of the original Greek text. Iambs may be the meter most closely associated with normal speech but it is not simply colloquial style written in iambics, it is poetic speech on a less elevated level than lyrics, but still on a higher stylistic level than regular speech.

Søren Ulrik Thomsen and I were convinced that it was wrong to use the traditional poeticizing style of Danish translations which have tended to eliminate the difference between iambic lines and choral lyrics. We felt that it was crucial to insist on the poetic and dramatic contrasts between the two levels of poetry in Greek tragedy, but we were also convinced that no Greek tragedy is like a modern realistic drama as seen on TV. Hence we did not want to use prose and colloquial style. We found it best to keep the translation in at least two different poetic modes. The non-lyrical passages were translated into rhythmical prose which makes the performance much more powerful than if written as prose, and appropriate since Greek tragedy deals with some of the central questions in human life: fate, honor, dignity, revenge, war. Such problems deserve, if anything does, to be handled with poetry and pathos. Furthermore, to separate the lyrical passages from the spoken lines we used 'free verse' (prose poetry) in the choral songs, sacrificing the triadic metrical structure, but preserving both the poetry and the dramatic tension at a higher level. By using these two modern types of poetry we hoped that the dramatic text would speak directly to the audience in the theater. This solution may not satisfy the expert, the Greek philologist, but then we do not translate for those who know Greek; for them we write learned commentaries on every little detail, details which the translator must incorporate in his translation so that he can do what many philologists never manage to do: express the drama on the stage which the text on the page is meant to represent.

How Ancient Greek Literature Reached Danish Readers

by
Minna Skafte Jensen

I.

That human beings speak a variety of languages has in Jewish-Christian history been understood as the result of God's wrath: it is his revenge for their outrageous construction of the tower of Babel. The art of translation, then, is mankind's attempt at a remedy for this and as such in itself caused by the conflict of Babel. In a famous commentary on the legend, Walter Benjamin moved the Babelic conflict from the confusion of languages to the problem of language itself: things and the words which referred to them corresponded directly in the garden of Eden, but their mutual relation has ever since been complicated. Accordingly, the difficulties of translation are not only caused by the distance between source and target, but just as much by the complexity of meaning inside each of the involved languages[1]; George Steiner speaks of "the essential implicitness of customary speech and writing"[2].

Greek antiquity was already far removed from paradise. In prehistoric times, translations of oral literature must have thrived - how else account for the formulas, themes and story-patterns in Hesiod and Homer which are known to have been imported from Anatolia, Mesopotamia and India? We must imagine a cultural traffic with singers and storytellers who were fluent in more than one language, and who assimilated into one tradition what they had learnt in another, presumably creating freely as they went along. It is not difficult to find comparisons in the modern world; e.g. many of Parry and Lord's Montenegrin informants were ethnic Al-

---

[1] Benjamin (1923) 1992; Gorlée 1994, 133-45.
[2] Steiner 1975, 276.

banians, performing in their own language as well as in Turkish and Serbo-Croatian[3]. Such multi-lingualism must have been current in many kinds of low-status activities - buying and selling, doing military service etc. - during the centuries of ancient culture, and oral literature, too, must have travelled without difficulty across borders of states and languages.

But with translation of literature in the ancient world, the passage from Greek to Latin is normally meant. Right from the earliest period of Latin literature, translation, imitation and emulation went hand in hand, covering the spectrum from the comedians' light-hearted utilisation of Greek new comedy to the highly refined game of intertextuality as cultivated by Catullus and Vergil. Also, the earliest theoreticians are found in Rome; I am referring, of course, to Cicero, Horace and St. Jerome. The two pagan authors agreed on the principle that the translator should not translate word for word, but take care to give the imported text a stylistically satisfactory Latin form. St Jerome, however, even though he accepted this as a general principle considered the Bible an exemption. The words of God could not be tampered with[4].

The oldest known example is Livius Andronicus' translation of the first verse of the *Odyssey*:

Virum mihi, Camena, insece versutum.

This is a remarkably successful version, being both *verbum e verbo* and *sensus e sensu:* First, Livius retains the important word-order of the source text, beginning with *virum* and thus keeping the title-function of this first word: The *Odyssey* is the epic of a man, just as the *Iliad* is about the wrath. Next, he has chosen to take from Roman religion the equivalent of the Greek muse, the Camena. And finally, he has found a translation of Homer's *polytropos,* which has both the same sense and the same metaphor: *versutus,* the hero of many turns, the cunning man. And all this takes place in a native Latin metre, the Saturnian. So in this first verse Livius has succeeded in creating a translation which offers his

---

[3] Parry & Lord 1954, 53-7.
[4] Cic. *De optimo genere oratorum* 14; Hor. A.P. 132-3; Hieron. Preface to the *Book of Esther.*

Latin readers the same content and a similar aesthetic experience as Homer's readers had had.

However, during the centuries following Livius Andronicus, the Roman poets gradually took over Greek metres, including the hexameter. Ennius, Lucretius, Cicero and Catullus - to mention only the most important names - elaborated this verse-form, and they did so both in translations from Greek and in new compositions inspired by the Greeks. By the time of Virgil and Horace the hexameter was a fully-fledged Roman metre. Horace translated the beginning of the *Odyssey* twice:

> rursus, quid virtus et quid sapientia possit,
> utile proposuit nobis exemplar Ulixen,
> qui domitor Troiae multorum providus urbes
> et mores hominum inspexit latumque per aequor,
> dum sibi, dum sociis reditum parat, aspera multa
> pertulit, adversis rerum inmersabilis undis[5].

The two verses first quoted state Horace's purpose, to demonstrate how Ulysses may be read as an example of virtue and wisdom. The four next verses translate Homer quite closely, beginning in the middle of v. 2. *Troies hieron ptoliethron eperse* is compressed into *domitor Troiae*; the Greek v. 3 is translated word for word, *multorum urbes et mores hominum inspexit*, but with the adjective *providus*, intelligent, added; Homer's v. 4 is in Horace *latumque per aequor aspera multa pertulit*, again very close to the original, except for the idiomatic *hon kata thymon*, in his soul, which is left out; and finally v. 5 is rendered by *dum sibi, dum sociis reditum parat*. In short, a close, almost pedantic translation. But just as Horace has added *providus*, he includes the words *adversis rerum inmersabilis undis*, summing up: Ulysses was a survivor, undrownable, however adverse waves he met. And these are not only the manifest waves of the sea, but also *undae rerum*, a sea of troubles.

His other rendering compresses the three first verses of the *Odyssey* into two:

> dic mihi, Musa, virum, captae post tempora Troiae

---

[5] Hor. *Ep.* 1.2.17-22.

qui mores hominum multorum vidit et urbes[6].

He has left out the end of Homer's v. 1 and the whole of 2, and he has not, as Livius, retained the effect of beginning the work with the word 'the man'. So paradoxically enough, even though he has retained from the Greek both the metre and the name of the goddess of inspiration, his translation is further removed from the source than was Livius'[7].

II.

During the history of Western Europe, no language has had a more important function in transmitting Greek classics to non-Greek readers than Latin. In the Middle Ages, classical Greek literature was known only through its Latin imitators. To stick to the same examples: Greek new comedy was influential in so far as people knew Plautus and Terence, and any idea of Homer could be had only by means of Roman poets such as Virgil and Statius. And when Renaissance poets began the long and laborious task of reconquering Greek epic for Western readers, it took the form of Latin translations. The Homeric poem which had the first and most numerous translations was *The Battle of Frogs and Mice*, simply because it was so much shorter than the *Iliad* and the *Odyssey*. In northern Europe, during the 16th through 18th centuries, 'Homer' meant hexameter translations by Eobanus Hessus or by Jacobus Micyllus and Joachimus Camerarius. Only with the onset of Romanticism did non-professional readers in any number begin to retrace the original in Greek.

Danes did not contribute significantly to this inter-European effort of translating Greek classics into Latin; the reason is, I think, that the Renaissance reached Scandinavia so late that the bulk of the job had been already completed when the Danish humanists entered the scene during the middle of the 16th century. But they certainly did contribute to the imitation- and emulation-activity by composing Latin poetry in almost all the known genres, and in some cases with considerable virtuosity. There is a beautiful metaphor for this: to invite the muses. The Greek muses made their entry into the Danish province of the learned repub-

---

[6] Hor. *A.P.* 141-2.
[7] Cf. Jacobsen 1958, 45-9.

lic with the full approval of Northern European centres of learning, such as Melanchthon's Wittenberg.

Translations into Danish of ancient classics to begin with meant translations from Latin, and they began roughly a century later than the first invitations of the muses. In 1639 Peder Jensen Roskilde translated Virgil's *Eclogues* into Danish verse. I quote his translation of the first lines of *Ecl.* 9:

Lycidas:
> Qvo te, Moeri, pedes? an, quo uia ducit in urbem?

Moeris:
> O Lycida, uiui peruenimus, aduena nostri
> (quod numquam ueriti sumus) ut possessor agelli
> diceret: 'haec mea sunt; ueteres migrate coloni.'
> nunc uicti, tristes, quoniam fors omnia uersat,
> hos illi (quod nec uertat bene) mittimus haedos.

Lycidas:
> Hvor vilt du reys' / O Moeri, / paa? /
> Til Byen som den Vey mon / gaa? /

Moeris:
> O Lycida, før hafve vi
> Ey fryctet for sligt Mytteri /
> I huilcket vi nu lefve maa /
> At fremmet Krigsmand tagr os fra
> Vor Eyedom / oc siger kort:
> Det mit er; packer eder bort.
> Saa er det Lyckens viis oc sed /
> At vende alting op oc ned;
> Som vi nu offvervundne maa
> Til Arrium bedrøffde gaa /
> Oc ham forære disse Kid /
> Saa gid hand der aff trifves lidt!

Just like Livius Andronicus, he chose a metre already familiar in his own language and building on stress. At the time of Jensen's translation, pastoral was a flourishing literary form in Danish, and the translator was thus in a position to offer Virgil's poems a natural place in an existing spectrum of genres. What he also did, and what is exemplified in the copied lines, was to make these enigmatic poems more understandable by incorporating into his translation the commentaries which had built up around Virgil's poetry ever since late antiquity. Even without knowing Danish, the reader can see the name of a certain Arrius in the translation which has no equivalent in the source; also the profession of this Arrius as a soldier, *Krigsmand*, is fetched from the commentaries, not from Virgil. So obviously, Jensen has felt that to transfer Virgil into Danish meant to take care both to make the poems understandable and aesthetically enjoyable[8].

The most monumental translation into Danish of a classical author from this period is Birgitte Thott's *Seneca* from 1658. It is explicitly addressed to the women of Denmark; Renaissance Latin was a men's language, and Birgitte Thott felt that as one of the few women who had been taught Latin she had a responsibility to let her fellow females into the world of learning. And now also the Greek classics began to make their entry; I mention especially Henrik Gerner's translation of Hesiod's *Works and Days* (1670).

The 17th century is also marked by the first theoretical treatises on vernacular metre and verse-forms. Early in the century Bertil Knudsen Aquilonius argued for a transposition of ancient quantitative metres into Danish; but - perhaps luckily - he was unsuccessful, and other metricians were instead discussing accent-rhythms, and of course inspired by Martin Opitz and other German theoreticians. This is also the period during which the topic referred to by Walter Benjamin reached us: Which of the many existing languages was the original one? In what language did God and Adam communicate in the garden of Eden?

The first attempts at Danish translations of Homer were composed in rhymed Alexandrian verse; they are from the end of the 18th century by Hans Seidelin and Laurits Sahl[9]. But they were outconquered by the hexameter, first as written by Poul Martin Møller and later by Christian Wilster. His Homer is the most famous Danish literary translation and

---

[8] Schiebe 1998, 9-13.
[9] Nielsen 1974, 27-35.

has in itself achieved the status of a classic.

Thus, the development in our country resembles the one in Rome: translators first chose a vernacular form, but gradually the hexameter was accepted into our aesthetics as a familiar verse-form, and as such the most natural choice for the translator of ancient Greek hexameters. The history has been different in the English-speaking world, presumably on the authority of Alexander Pope.

But independently of the ways in which translations have been made, their importance was tremendous for the inspiration Western Europe had from Ancient Greece. Reception of the Greek classics as compared to the Latin ones has taken place largely by means of translations. And this mediation has been extremely successful: generations of readers have been touched and moved. This has happened notwithstanding the fact that the texts were not original. It might even be considered if it did not happen because of the translations, that the translators' efforts to meet the readers' language, culture and taste have actually helped readers appreciate the works.

III.

It is easy to say what is a bad translation: it is one that makes mistakes, being made by a translator without a sufficient mastery of the source language. It is much more complicated to describe what is a good translation. The ideal - which to my mind was achieved by Livius Andronicus, at least in his rendering of the first verse of his source - transplants both form and content, both message and connotations into the target language. But in general, all kinds of factors are at work to make that impossible.

Where Greek classics are concerned, there are some typical problems connected with the source texts. How original are they in the first place?

According to Roman Jakobson there are three kinds of translation: intralingual, interlingual and intersemiotic[10], and I shall dwell a little on the importance of intralingual translation in this connection. Many of our Greek classics have been intralingually translated already in their earliest phase: I am referring to the fact that they have been transmitted to us in writing, whereas archaic and classical Greek literature was largely composed orally, or even if composed in writing meant to be per-

---

[10] Jakobsen 1966; Steiner 1975, 260-61.

formed orally. The process from oral composition to written text meant a loss of orality, aurality and visuality. Our written texts are mutilated, lacking the performing voice and body, the whole register of shifting intonations, mimicry, gestures, scenography, dance, music etc. It also meant a fixing of what was otherwise flexible, in the loss of the direct contact between poet/performer and audience.

The texts gained something in the process as well: the accessibility for an abstract readership, unknown to the poet, even future readers such as ourselves; and it offered the readers the chance of other ways of reception, perhaps most importantly the possibility of reading in-depth offered to the solitary reader at the desk, reading quietly and patiently, consulting handbooks etc.

As for the target language and the target audience, it is a commonplace that there is nothing in the modern world to compare to a Greek performance, normally part of a religious festival, in which an audience had a collective experience. Even performance in the modern world, such as theatrical staging, is basically different from Greek performance. But I want to stress this fact more than it is normally done. I shall argue that the greatest problem in translating Greek classics into Danish lies in the distance between the social contexts in which literature belongs.

Even when we read a Greek classic in the original, we are, I submit, translating[11]. At least when we are reading in class - and I continue using Homer as the example. We read his verses aloud, but we do so translating his quantitative rhythm into a modern system of accentuating. We discuss word for word, phrase for phrase, explaining as we proceed. We feel that we are reading Greek; but is not it a more precise description to say that we translate? interlingually and intralingually, substituting Danish explanations for the Greek source. During the process we lose the music of the verse and the drive of the narrative, but win the qualities the slow reader gets. Paradoxically, it might be argued that modern readers understand Homer better than his first audience ever did.

On the other hand, the modern Dane sitting in an armchair reading Homer in translation just for the fun of it, is in some respects closer to the poet's ancient audience than the philologist studying the Greek o-

---

[11] Cf. Steblin-Kamenskij 1973, 13-15.

riginal. The non-professional reader stands a good chance of spontaneously experiencing the grandeur of the overall composition, and of feeling the rhythm of Homer's narrative, the shifts in tempo, the variations between pathos and bathos, tragedy and lighter moods.

But our ways of reading the *Iliad* and the *Odyssey* - both the slow philological study and the quicker reading of a translation - would have astonished the poet, had he heard of it.

I am not, of course, arguing that it is unimportant to read Greek classics in their own language, or that it is better to read them in translation. The two kinds of reading are both definitely far from the 'original', each in its own way. And of course, the reader of a translation is at the mercy of the translator. In some ways, a translation demands more of the reader than an original: The reader of a translation must both be willing to accept the translated work as literature in its own terms, and suspiciously remember that it is a translator's interpretation of an original, that is, even more than literature in general, a multi-layered text.

Just as I enjoy different poets, I think it is a richness that translators do not follow the same rules, some keeping the strangeness, the 'Entfremdung' of the process, others working to familiarise. Various translators have their strengths and weaknesses in various aspects. In the history of Danish translation we do not, to my knowledge, have any translators keeping so closely to the source language at the cost of the target language as did Friedrich Hölderlin in his Sophocles-versions; but it is thought-provoking that exactly the professional artist among the translators, the author and philosopher Villy Sørensen, is the most ardent adherent of keeping very closely to the original[12]. For a small language as Danish, it is a remarkable fact that currently we have, for instance, three translators of ancient Greek hexameter poetry performing their task in three very different ways: Lene Andersen, Otto Steen Due and Kai Møller Nielsen.

So in paying homage to the tower of Babel and the wonders it brought us, I especially stress my admiration for the subtle and varied art of the translators.

---

[12] Sørensen 1996-7.

References

Benjamin, W. (1923) 1992
  The task of the translator, in: WB: *Illuminations*. Edited by H. Arendt. Trl. by H. Zohn. London, 70-82.

Brower, R.A. (1959) 1966
  On Translation. New York.

Gorlée, D.L. 1994
  Semiotics and the Problem of Translation. With Special Reference to the Semiotics of Charles S. Peirce (Approaches to Translation Studies 12). Amsterdam.

Jacobsen, E. 1956
  Translation, A Traditional Graft. An Introductory Sketch with a Study of Marlowe's Elegies. Copenhagen.

Jakobsen, R. (1959) 1966
  On linguistic aspects of translation, in: Brower (1959) 1966, 232-9.

Nielsen, K. Møller 1974
  Homeroversættelser og Heksameterdigte. Odense.

Parry, M. & A.B. Lord (edd.) 1954
  Serbocroatian Heroic Songs. Collected by MP, edited and translated by ABL. Vol. I. Cambridge and Belgrade.

Roskilde, Peder Jensen (1639) 1909
  Vergils Bucolica, ed. V.J. von Holstein Rathlou (Studier fra Sprog- og Oldtidsforskning 78). Copenhagen.

Schiebe, M. Wifstrand 1998
  Vergil og Tityrus (Studier fra Sprog- og Oldtidsforskning 332). Copenhagen.

Steblin-Kamenskij, M.I. 1973
  The Saga Mind. Trl. by K.H. Ober. Odense.

Steiner, G. 1975
  After Babel. Aspects of Language and Translation. Oxford.

Sørensen, V. 1996-7
  Seneca - en hofmand, der hellere ville være vismand, *Standart* 10.5, 15.

Translating the Bible

by
Lene Andersen

The following observations on the topic "Translating the Bible" are based on my membership of the committee which in the 1980es worked on a new translation of the New Testament into Danish.

This was part of a new translation of the whole Bible, organized by the Ministry of Ecclesiastical Affairs and by the Danish Bible Society; it was authorized in 1992 by the Queen, Margrethe II, in her capacity of being Head of the Danish National Church.

My observations are also based on my being member of the committee translating the Apocryphal Books of the Old Testament, authorized in 1998.

My task in the New Testament project was a double one: First together with another translator to produce the basic translation of some of The New Testament letters, namely the Letter to the Hebrews and the so-called Catholic Letters (in short: the non-Pauline letters). Secondly to be a consultant on the Greek language. Because I was educated as a classical philologist it was my obligation to supplement the New Testament scholars' special knowledge of Koine Greek with a broader knowledge of ancient Greek language.

During the translation of the Apocryphal Books of The Old Testament, written - and with a single exception only known - in the Greek of The Septuaginta, I was one of the translators bringing about the basic translation of *Sapientia,* The Wisdom of Solomon.

Both the translation of the New Testament and that of the Apocrypha was produced by a group of scholars, but they were organized in different ways.

In the following I shall deal with some aspects of the history of translating the Bible into Danish, with the necessity of rather frequent new translations of ancient texts, with the special conditions for Bible translation compared with most other translation, and with the question: new translation versus revision. In addition I shall comment on the organization of the two above mentioned translation tasks.

Before 1992 we had in Denmark a Bible consisting of an Old Testament authorized in 1931 and a New Testament authorized in 1948. Both translations, however, were several years earlier than that: The old Testament of 1931 is an adaptation of an unauthorized version from 1910, and the New Testament of 1948 was translated in the thirties.

For many years the translations of the two testaments have been out of step with each other: The previous New Testament translation was made in 1907 and went at first together with an Old Testament translated in 1871. We have to look back to 1740 to find an edition of the two testaments authorized simultaneously, and that was as a matter of fact a revision, not a new translation.

It is of course much to prefer to have the whole Bible translated simultaneously with a common linguistic caracter, and this became possible with the translation of 1992.

Admittedly, the Apocrypha of the Old Testament were first added in 1998. It was however just a short slip and the translators were among the same translators who had translated the canonic books.

Looking at the history of the Danish Bible from the Reformation in 1536, we see that there are generally 50 to 100 years between the appearance of new translations or revisions.

These rather frequent renewals are made necessary partly because the target language, Danish, is changing, but that is not the only reason.

It is well known that we read literature not only 50 and 100 years old, but even older without difficulty. Just think of Hans Christian Andersen. Perhaps a word or an idea or a notion needs explanation, but the language as a whole is still fresh and comprehensible.

The reason why translated texts so soon become obsolete is, I think, due to the character and demands of the translation process itself:

The translator of course has to be absolutely loyal to the text translated. First and foremost he has to understand it accurately, and when he reproduces it, to try to express as many of its subtleties as possible.

The translator must be very attentive to the target language too. It is part of his work to listen again and again to his own sentences: "Is this idiomatic? Is this how we put it in Danish?"

This means, that the translator seldom uses an original way of speaking. There is imbedded in the task of the translator a tendency to normalize. This means that the translation is often marked by its time in a narrower and more conservative way than is an original text of the same time. Therefore, translations of important texts need to be replaced by new ones with intervals.

To meet objections, I hurry to admit that there are exceptions: Instances of translations so good that they have become classics themselves and have entered the literature of a nation along with the original works. But I am afraid that these are happy exeptions.

The Bible translation of Martin Luther is a bright example. It is a brilliant work of one person and has had enormous influence.

More astonishing is it that the English Bible-translation from the beginning of the 17. century, "the Authorized Version", has had similar qualities and influence. And yet it was made by a committee with about 50 persons, and was furthermore a revision of an earlier work.

In Denmark we have a translation of Homer made by Christian Wilster in 1836 and 1837. This translation has become *the* Homer in Denmark. It is in itself a piece of literature of its own entity, unsurpassed since then. Only now it is very likely to get a successor on the same level, Otto Steen Due's brand-new translation of The Iliad.

Translating Greek works of literature from antiquity you meet with certain problems which I think are well known to all of us: The main difficulty is to bridge the gap not only in language, but in time and culture which separates us from the author of the original text and his situation.

Solving these problems demands of course great linguistic ability, philological exactness, knowledge of historical and cultural matters, a wide literary horizon regarding both languages, and, if not artistic gifts, then at least aesthetical fantasy and judgement.

Accomplishing such a task you normally enjoy great freedom. You are first and foremost responsible to your own conscience as a scholar and a respectable person. Accepting this responsibility you have the full authority to make the choices between alternative interpretations and expressions which constantly meet the translator. And you have the freedom to mould the style.

There are examples of private translations of the Bible where translators have had the opportunity to work in this way.

But when you prepare a translation of the Bible with an official authorization in mind, that is a version which can and must be used in the churches, the circumstances are different. Before it can be recommended to authorization, the translation must be approved by the ecclesiastical authorities, who will listen to and decide on opinions given by the theological faculties of the universities, by religious groupings, by especially invited readers and by the public. Under these circumstances the translator does not work on his own responsibility alone and has not the authority to make the final decisions so as to secure that general meaning and style which he finds proper. As a natural consequence Bible translations will appear anonymously. Other special conditions too manifest themselves:

One special fact relating to Bible translation is that you translate a text which is indispensable. Not many texts from antiquity are indispensable in that absolute and practical way.

From a historical and cultural point of view it is of course very desirable that as much as possible of ancient literature is translated. But the supply of translations is generally governed by the interest and commitment of individual scholars, artists etc. The exception, again, are the Homeric poems, the reading of which is officially prescribed in the Danish grammar school.

The Bible in the mother tongue is absolutely indispensable in that plain and simple meaning, that the Danish National Church can not function without it. Services can simply not be performed. Alternate readings from the Bible form a great part of the liturgy of services and other ecclesiastical ceremonies, and the remaining liturgical elements will either consist of or be deeply marked by the wording of the biblical texts. Add to this the use of the Bible in countless types of education together with the private and joint use of it by people in the Evangelic-Lutheran creed, to whom the principle "sola scriptura", the scripture as the only authority, is crucial.

Another special fact relating to Bible translation is, that, whether you like it or not, you always translate in a tradition of translators.

The Bible has been translated since antiquity, to Danish (broadly speaking) since the Reformation. These translations have been used in the congregations officially and privately through centuries.

The texts prescribed for sermons have been heard year after year. The texts forming part of the rituals for baptism, communion and wedding have been stored in people's minds through their lifetime.

Quotations from the Bible are ubiquitous in our hymnbook, and concise wordings from the Bible are often of great importance to people in everyday life and in critical situations. They also, as is well known, are found everywhere in literature and in familiar quotations. Neither translators nor readers come to a new translation of the Bible without previous knowledge.

Translating biblical texts, you must be aware of these connections and make up your mind about them. At the same time they must not be allowed to paralyse you. That would of course in consequence mean abandoning the project.

But you will be wise to count on strong feelings and reactions when biblical texts are translated and to envisage that the expectations are often inconsistent with one another: They may include the wish for a Bible in a modern, easily understood language ("Why is the Bible to be read in an oldfashioned, obsolete language?") as well as the wish for the recognizable, for consideration for the tradition ("How dare you alter the Bible?"). Or the expectations may be directed by specific dogmatic conceptions or religious attitudes.

The translator has to operate somewhere between these contrasts. One must add that when the work is the work of a committee, the same kinds of tensions may easily be found *inside* the group, and that different points of view on scholarly and dogmatical questions as well as different wills will assert themselves (sometimes vigorously).

In the following I shall concentrate on our latest Danish Bible translation:

It started in the 1970es as a much needed new translation of the Old Testament, especially demanded by an altered textual basis.

Furthermore, many Old Testament scholars estimated the existant translation as being romantized and as artificially patinated.

Only in the middle of the 1980es did the idea turn up to make a new New Testament translation in order to obtain a total, simultaneously made, translation of the whole Bible, the first since 1740, as above mentioned.

After a pilot project, the work was formally begun in 1986. The work was officially ordained by the Ministry of Ecclesiastical Affairs, by which the editors were appointed. They in turn were authorized to appoint further translators etc.

The realization was given into the charge of the Danish Bible Society which had originally fostered the idea and taken the initiative. A numerous and complex board was then made:

The translation was made by 16 translators, working two by two.

At their disposal were nine consultants with various special knowledge for example literature, liturgy, hymnology, pedagogy, the Danish language, the Greek language. The consultants functioned when asked about specific problems and were obliged to go through the whole material of translations and comment on them.

The translations were further evaluated by the editorial committee consisting of five persons. Two of these were leading editors, who had to make the final decision if necessary.

Proposed amendments, alterations, modifications and new proposed amendments went to and fro between all those people several times, and in 1989 a provisional translation could be presented to the public. It was accessible for about a year and everybody was invited to comment on it.

The use of so many translators was caused partly by the wish to do the job very quickly, partly by the wish to involve so many persons, that both the scientific demands were properly met and various ecclesiastical points of view were represented from the beginning of the work.

Most of the translators were theologians from the universities, professors, assistant professors etc. Also some clergymen, bishops and vicars, who had contributed to New Testament scholarship, took part in the work.

The basic translation was in fact made in an admirably short time. But from then on the progress of the work was more complicated.

There was a long way from the translators' desk to the binding decisions by the editors' board.

Several useful and inspiring plenary meetings were held, where general questions were discussed, but details could of course not be discussed and settled in these great assemblies.

A substantial complex of problems was the problems of concordance. It will always be crucial in a translation of the New Testament, beeing as it is a collection of the texts with a common theme, but with different personalities as their authors. The problems of concordance, of course, were multiplied by the large number of translators.

Another partly related complex of problems caused some trouble, because in this case scholarly and religious interests sometimes clashed:

I think of the Old Testament citations in the New Testament. The improved textual basis for the Hebrew (Masoretic) text of the Old Testament and in the whole the legitimate claim to stick to the Hebrew text, sometimes caused discrepancies in relation to the citations in the New Testament, whose textual basis in many of these cases is a *Greek* Old Testament, especially the Septuaginta.

It is, of course, not a happy situation, if you turn from a citation in the New Testament to the Old Testamnent and then find something else. On the other hand, it would be utterly incorrect to go beyond either the Hebrew or the Greek text in order to obtain agreement in citations.

I am confident concerning the Old Testament and I know concerning the New Testament, that the philological and scholarly demands have not been set aside in the making of the translation.

But much effort has been given to harmonize, where crucial questions turn up.

This together with a tendency in the editorial board to favour the consideration for tradition in the New Testament translation has brought about that we ended up with a somewhat conservative translation without striking renewals. Many people like this, of course, while others would have preferred something more radical and therefore might think that a mountain of organization has given birth to a healthy, but little mouse.

The fact mentioned above that translation always is made within a tradition together with the far-reaching consideration for tradition in the actual translation is apt to forward a reflection on translation versus revision. Should the New Testament from 1992 be caracterized as a revision rather than as a new translation?

As I see it, the question of translation versus revision is not a question of the extent or degree of alteration.

It is a question of the working method. What is the basis? Is it the original Greek text or is it the existing translation? A revision will take its starting point in the translation and will in cases of unsatisfactory language, style, consequence, or the like go to the original text and see, if it is possible to amend as desired.

The New Testament from 1992 *is* really a new *translation*. This was the object defined by the Ministry of Ecclesiastic Affairs and the Danish Bible Society:

The translation must be made on the basis of the so-called Nestle Edition 26 with a constant view to the variant readings brought there. And on this basis the work has been done. The translators have honestly and throughout worked on the basis of the Greek text.

The question however can be asked if we have got the full benefit from this great work, or if the same result could have been obtained by the simpler procedure of a revision. The answer, so to speak, is blowing in the wind.

To me, however, considering the comprehensive basic work, it would have been desirable to go further to achieve not only a decent translation and a text more easily understood than that of 1948, but also an even more penetrating and precise text.

There are in the basic work from the translators many unused proposals, which I think in some cases very well could have been used or in other cases could have deserved further consideration.

In the final analysis, the Danish New Testament from 1948 has got a reasonable successor. And the translation offers a fair modernization. I am sure this can be justly said, and I think it deserves appreciation. The text has become easier to understand for many people and nobody should have reason to feel alien to the New Testament in this version.

Finally a few words about the organization of the translation of the Apocryphal or Deuterocanonical Books of the Old Testament, which was different from that of the New Testament:

The major books were divided into three sections:

1) What we call the legendary ones (Judith, Tobit)
2) The wisdom literature (The wisdom of Jesus Son of Sirach, The Wisdom of Solomon)
3) The historical books (The 1. and 2. Books of the Maccabees).

To every section were attached 5 to 6 persons including the three editors who joined all the three groups and worked as translators too.

One person made a basic translation for a whole text or a greater part of a text, and this was discussed in the group word by word, line by line, until agreement was obtained.

It was a slow process, but it gave good results. The close and constant collaboration favoured the mutual understanding of each translator's intentions and allowed a thorough argumentation leading to great precision in style and expression.

In one other way the work with the Apocrypha is different from the work with the canonical texts: There is no great interest in it. The Apocrypha are only known by few people in Denmark and play no part in clerical life. Therefore, there are no strong feelings connected with their form and wording. The weight of tradition is not so great, which gives a greater freedom to the translators.

Here again the translators are anonymous in order to signify that the authorized text is nobody's personal work but is brought about in an interplay between several persons and endorsed by them to be authorized by others.

For scholars accustomed to translating ancient literature alone and on one's own responsibility it is a special experience to take part in teamwork like this, translating the Bible. It could occasionally cause frustration when you had to give up bright solutions (your own or others), but first and foremost it was attractive, inspiring and stimulating thanks to the great expertise accumulated.

---

* *I thank senior Master Niels Munck for having revised my English.*

Translations and Classical Civilization in the Danish Gymnasium

by
Chr. Gorm Tortzen

Translations in the Danish educational system

It may seem a bit impolite – in the present context – to point out that in the Danish educational system translations play but a minor rôle. At the primary school level as well as at the secondary, the *gymnasium*, books on almost all subjects are written by Danish authors, mostly by teachers practicing themselves. Nowadays, university teachers very seldom write books intended for the gymnasium – and some would say, too seldom for the university as well. At the university level translations are also very rare, since all students are expected to know at least English – and to some extent German and French. This means that in the gymnasium almost all books are Danish both as far as the language is concerned and in their educational conception.

This is a very fortunate situation, I think, since it is essential for elementary as well as more advanced education that the problems of a specific subject, (scientific, linguistic or literary) are presented from a point of view similar to that of the student. I am not sure that the Danish educational authorities fully understand how privileged the school system is to have writers and editors who still find it worthwhile to write school books in the native language of the student. This is the most effective way to consolidate the Danish educational traditions and habits, and there is no indication that this should change in future.

At the universities it is quite the opposite, as you can see from the bibliographies handed out from most institutes: The books recommended are almost all in foreign languages, and since there is no academic prestige in writing university textbooks in Denmark, American books (with their educational traditions) are dominant at many university institutes.

Classical Civilization in the gymnasium

From these considerations one might conclude that the literary genre 'translation' is of no interest in the Danish educational system. This is not correct, of course. In school, translations are used to some extent by teachers of modern literature and history, but the main consumers are the students of a subject unique for the Danish gymnasium: *Oldtidskundskab*, normally translated *Classical Civilization* or more correctly *Greek Culture*. Since 1903, when classical Greek as a language became an optional subject only, all Danish students have been taught Greek civilization from translations of Greek epic, from the philosophers, historians, dramatists and orators. When the new subject was introduced many classical teachers were appalled by the idea of teaching Greek culture without Greek language. Some of them resigned in protest, and Dr. Kazialis' description of the reactions from teachers in today's Greece when forced to work on new conditions is comparable to the frustrations of many Danish teachers in the years after 1903. Today we all agree that M.Cl. Gertz, professor of classical philology in Copenhagen, was foresighted when he advised the Ministry of Education to give up the linguistic part of Greek in the curriculum for the many and save the Greek language for the few, in order to communicate Greek literature and art to all students. This maneuvre saved Greek at the secondary school level, and even today appr. 125 students pass the examinations in Classical Greek (only a little less than total number in 1903), while all their fellow students (appr. 20,000) take Classical Civilization, three lessons a week for one year. In the other Scandinavian countries classical Greek is almost non existant in schools, and no Classical Civilization has substitued the loss.

The market for translations

Every Danish undergraduate has read some books of Homer and a dialogue of Plato (Homer and Plato are in fact the only authors in the curriculum of the Danish gymnasium that are compulsory – no Danish authors have got such a privilege). Furthermore, two dramas, some Herodotus or Thucydides, a couple of speeches by Lysias or some other writers. This has some interesting implications. Since the curriculum consists in appr. 300 pages of Greek prose, drama, epics and lyrics in translation, it means that the 20,000 Danish students graduating every year have read all together six million pages of Greek literature – plus mythology, history of art etc. etc.

This means that there is quite a market for Greek authors in translation – contrary to the Latin authors – and that Denmark compared to Sweden and Norway is much better off. Classical Civilization is no doubt the main reason for the popularity of Ancient Greek culture in Denmark and for the considerable production of books on classical themes and texts. Some would even say that the subject Classical Civilization is fundamental for the success of the Danish university studies of Antiquity as well.

Translators' Practise

For 25 years I have taught Classical Civilization, using the existing translations. Since I began teaching, the selection of titles available has grown from a dozen old standard editions to several hundreds. We now have translation of all 'major' authors – either whole works or selections.

Some of the standard translations are good, really good – others are not, and I shall venture to make a list of some rather subjective observations concerning Danish translations of classical texts.

To translators of modern languages some of the following remarks may seem a little strange.

I do not think it more difficult (or easier) to translate from classical Greek than from modern. But while most modern translators have been professionally trained in transferring one language into another, the classical philologist is normally an autodidact in the *ars interpretandi,* since this difficult work is not included in the normal university curriculum. Furthermore, the classicist has to free himself from the awful habits, one gets while doing the so called 'unseens from Greek and Latin' in school – *translation* is here a real misnomer! There are also serious stilistic problems due to the puristic, awkward and utterly outdated stock vocabulary of the Greek and Latin dictionaries written a century (and a half) ago. These achaisms have been trained at an early age and together with standard solutions of transferring Greek or Latin syntax into Danish they constitute af sort of philological jargon. Too many translations show that these bad habits are not so easy to get rid of as one might think.

The ideal translation of a classical text for educational purposes

I have six unscientific points to make about the ideal classical translation for educational purposes – and in a way also for other translations meant for the public.

1. Relevance to the supposed reader

The translator must have made up his mind about whom the translation is intended for. He must never forget that students in the gymnasium are about 18 years old when they study Classical Civilization – and not all aspects of Greek literature seem equally relevant to them.

Some texts are essential or important to a general reader (e.g. Homer, some of the Platonic dialogues, some of the dramas), others are not. Since the translator normally works on his own, *con amore*, and with no financial support, he must ask himself (or rather a colleague) whether or not this text is suited for school purposes. It does not mean that it should not be translated, only that it should be done in another way, perhaps.

2. No technical language

In the gymnasium (as elsewhere), most readers have no Greek, and therefore the translation must not presuppose any knowledge of Greek, e.g. the technical terms often found in translations of philosophy.

3. Legibility

When reading the translation, the reader must always have the impression that the text is a trustworthy rendering of an ancient writer and not a philologist's pedantic version. Too many old Danish translations are more or less illegible for a non-philologist, because the translators mistakenly try to render all the Greek linguistic niceties of the particles and the genitive absolute.

Another pitfall is the fear of boring the reader. Some of the new Danish translations of Aristophanes are not as funny as the translators think they are, and their language is pathetically outdated after a few years because many 'comtemporary' words and expressions turned out to be ephemeral.

4. Style

The text is old but the translation must look new. Like other modern languages, Danish constantly changes; some expressions become outdated and are replaced by new ones. Unfortunately, Danish philologists are rather conservative – at least from a linguistic point of view – and many translations are in fact a bit oldfashioned the day they appear.

Leo Hjortsø, the *primus inter pares* among the classical translators for more than 30 years, once said that every 25 years all translations should be collected and burned all together. It is a little drastic, but it has some truth in it.

But only some truth. The fact is that the readability of a translation depends not only on the age of the translation (or of the translator), but rather on the translator's skill in translation and his ear for his native language at its present stage.

5. Lay out and price

It is not enough just to make a good translation. There must be an introduction and some notes explaining – not everything but e.g. ancient names or important notions and ideas that an average reader (18 years old or more) does not understand or fails to recognize. Too many translators forget that the reader has not worked with the text for years – and does not intend to do it either.

Another point too often neglected is the lay-out. In an age when the supposed readers watch TV for more hours than they read, the book must look interesting. Even today too many Danish schoolbooks are printed in a way that makes you wonder whether the editor actually wants the students to get bored before they open the book – and turn it aside when they look inside: Small print, a clumsy lay-out, poor pictures, if any. 'Due to the price!' editors excuse themselves. I find it very important, that a text that has survived, say 2,500 years, is presented with some respect. On the other hand, if a schoolbook is expensive no one can afford to buy 30 copies for the class, and since the issue is normally 2,000 copies it is difficult for the editor to make much money on classics.

6. Bestsellers?

In the market of Danish translations of classics there are some real bestsellers, e.g. 'The Red Plato' – It's only the binding that is red. The inside is highly conservative. For more than 60 years this book has been *the Plato*. Its picture of Socrates goes back to the Age of Enlightenment and could be described as a *passio sancti Socratis*: *Apology, Crito* and the end of *Phaedo*; later modernized with a section of *Meno* – 'for the more clever classes' as the preface puts it.

The most read editions of *Antigone* and *Medea* are highly problematic in their interpretation of the text; the selections from Herodotus are rather one-eyed etc. etc. I am sorry to say it, but as far as I know there is no direct correlation between quality and popularity. Some of the most popular (i.e. most commonly read) translations should have been maculated years ago. Other much better editons are seldom used. Teachers are extremely conservative, and the popularity of an edition seems often to depend on what the Ancient Greeks call *kairos*, the right (and lucky) moment.

Classical translations in future

But generally speaking, today the quality of textbooks intended for *Classical Civilization* is much better than 25 years ago and, as mentioned before, the selection of classical translations in Denmark has never been bigger than today. Fortunately there is more to come:

We have just seen the new Homer translated by prof. Otto Steen Due; a society of Xenophon lovers are working on *The Complete Xenophon*, part of which has already been printed. The *Memorabilia* and the *Hieron* are to follow next. New selections from Plato, Aristotle's *Metaphysics* etc. etc. are forthcoming. Recently – after decades of neglect – translations from Roman literature have been made such as Virgil, Lucretius and Cicero's *Philippics*.

Time for planning

In Denmark the classical tradition and book production of classical literature in translation depends on a very sensitive symbiosis between *con amore* translators, the educational system and the editors – and sometimes between the editors and financial funds. The result has been many and often good new translations, but until now with no general plan.

I therefore suggest that some one should list the most urgent *desider-*

ata – e.g. a new Thucydides – find someone capable of translating, and make them do it.

If the art of translating the ancient texts into modern Danish shall exist in future we have to start planning now.

Bibliography

All Danish translations of classics up to 1991 are registered in:

Elkjær, Kjeld og Per Krarup, *Danmark og Antiken*, 2nd ed. Copenhagen 1968 (translations from the late 18th century to 1967).

Kristensen, Birgit Juul og Joan Majlund Kristensen, *Danmark og antikken 1968-1979. En bibliografi over 12 års dansksproget litteratur om den klassiske oldtid.* Copenhagen 1982.

Andersen, Flemming Gorm, *Danmark og antikken 1980-1991. En bibliografi over 12 års dansksproget litteratur om den klassiske oldtid.* Copenhagen 1994.

European Literature in Translation: Research at the Center for the Greek Language

by
Takis Kayalis

My purpose is to present a set of research projects on literature in translation, which we have developed at the Center for the Greek Language in Thessaloniki; some of these projects have already been completed and published, while others are still underway. I will present each project briefly, but I will also touch on some broader questions and problems which I hope may furnish ground for discussion amongst us.

Let me first provide some information about the institution I represent. The Center for the Greek Language was founded by the Greek Ministry of Education five years ago; it is headed by the distinguished classicist, translator and literary critic Dimitris Maronitis and, as I already mentioned, is based in Thessaloniki. The Center functions as an independent research institute and, at the same time, as the Ministry of Education's advisory and co-ordinating agent on issues of language policy. It has four divisions, covering the fields of lexicography, linguistics, applied linguistics and language and literature (there is also a separate program on translation from ancient to modern Greek, which is directed by Professor Maronitis). The projects I will present here are all supervised by the division of language and literature, which I have been directing since the Center's inception, with the collaboration of Prof. Nassos Vayenas of the University of Athens, who is the division's academic advisor.

Although some of our work is concerned exclusively with Modern Greek literature —for example, we have undertaken the completion and publication of the monumental Cavafy Bibliography which Dimitris Daskalopoulos has been preparing for almost twenty years— most of our programs focus on literature in translation and fall into two general categories: Modern Greek literature in translation and European and World literature in Greek translation.

Beginning with the first category, let me make a brief comment on our position concerning research of Modern Greek literature in translation. In recent years, we are experiencing in Greece an increasing sense of urgency concerning the translatability and promotion of our literature abroad. This sense is widespread in the media and state agencies as well as the literary community, and is certainly connected to the awareness that interest in Modern Greek literature has radically decreased during the last decade or two, especially in European and American metropolitan centers, both in the academic environment and in terms of the general reading public. Despite this urgency, or perhaps because of it, and of the absurd notions and claims that sometimes accompany it, initiatives for the promotion of Greek literature abroad often lack concrete objectives and are executed in a haphazard fashion. That is to say, Greek literature is sometimes represented by mediocre examples, promoted by unqualified entrepreneurs, translated in a manner that no one would care to read, and published by clandestine publishers, in subsidized volumes that reach few bookstores and even fewer readers.

Our intervention in this thorny field is based on three principles: first, we are committed to serious academic research and, in particular, to projects which lay foundations and open possibilities for further work. Second, we support highly qualified foreign scholars, who have demonstrated their capacity not only to produce excellent work, but also to make it available to serious readers in their countries. And third, we strongly promote the establishment of communication and cooperation with other peripheral cultures in Europe. In our understanding, a major part of the problem is the rigid orientation towards the few metropolitan Centres and the consequent neglect of cultural conducts that promise far more balanced and fruitful exchange. In other words, we believe that initiatives like the seminar on Translators and Translations, which establish direct communication between cultures that know little of each other can be far more productive and mutually beneficial than grand schemes which aim to conquer the world and usually end with a strong after taste of provincialism.

Our work in this area so far consists of three projects: first, we supported Dr. Hero Hokwerda's research on contemporary Greek prose, which led to the production of an anthology of twenty-five short stories, translated in Dutch by Dr. Hokwerda himself (the volume was published in Amsterdam by Meulenhoff publisher in 1997). Second, we invited Dr. David Ricks of King's College, London University to produce a major anthology of Modern Greek poetry and prose in English. This project was completed last year and the anthology will soon be published in England by Peter Owen. It contains old and new translations of two hundred and fifty texts by fifty authors, from Solomos and Makriyannis to Mihalis Ganas and Rea Galanaki. Thus next year we will have the first comprehensive anthology of 19th and 20th-century Greek literature in English translation, a book which we expect will be widely used in the academic environment and, hopefully, will also attract the interest of non-academic readers.

Our third initiative is sponsored by the Greek Ministry of Culture and took off last year. This project's purpose is to thoroughly record and evaluate existing translations from Greek literature in ten languages (or, in some cases, groups of languages). At this stage we have created research teams in Italy and Spain, and in the course of the next four years we will continue with Bulgarian, Dutch, French, German, Portuguese, Romanian, Serbo-Croatian, and Turkish. Each team begins with the collection of full bibliographical data and proceeds with evaluation; our primary concern is to specify which translations are functional today, as literary texts, in each language and also to locate important works which have not been translated in the particular language or whose existing translations are not functional, for historical or aesthetic reasons. Researchers are also asked to look into more mundane issues, such as the actual distribution and circulation of published translations, the prestige and potential of subsidized publishers, particular reading interests and opportunities arising in each cultural environment, and so on. Our purpose is to create a complete collection of data for each target language, which will be useful to prospective translators and researchers, but also to state agencies which so far had to subsidize translations of Greek literature abroad based mainly on rumours or instinct.

Our work has developed more extensively in the second area I mentioned earlier, that is: Foreign literature in Greek translation. This field is equally difficult to handle, since it has largely escaped scholarly and critical attention in Greece, for a variety of reasons, ranging from traditional ethnocentric inhibition to theoretical inertia. In 1997 we organized a symposium on literary translation in Thessaloniki, which led to the publication of a volume of nine essays, on historical and theoretical problems as well as on the translation of specific major texts (such as Shakespeare's *Sonnets*, Proust's *A la recherche du temps perdu* and Ezra Pound's *Cantos*). We also supported and published last year a research project of Lefteris Papaleontiou, a colleague at the University of Cyprus, who surveyed two hundred and fifty periodicals, journals and newspapers and produced a bibliography of literary translations published in Asia Minor, Cyprus and Egypt from 1880 to 1930. This important work unearths and makes accessible a completely forgotten tradition and, simultaneously, a cosmopolitan Greek culture whose associations are quite impressive. So now even a complete illiterate on things Danish, like myself, can attempt to impress expert readers announcing for example that prose by Herman Bang, Steen Steensen Blicher, Jens Peter Jakobsen, Johannes Joergensen and Henrik Pontoppidan was translated in Greek and published in Alexandria and Smirni between 1912 and 1922.

Let me now turn to two other major projects we are working on. Last year, we were invited by the Ministry of Education to produce a textbook, for the instruction of European Literature at the second class of the Lyceum. The book was edited by Prof. Vayenas and myself, with the cooperation of three colleagues with extensive experience in the secondary education, and was used during the past academic year, in which European Literature was taught for the first time in Greece. It is an anthology of 78 poems and short stories in translation, from Dante to contemporary authors like Zbigniew Herbert and Drago Yancar, with a general introduction and critical commentaries for each text. One of the major problems we had to face, in preparing this anthology, was the definition of European literature itself. We opted for the broadest possible definition, and so we managed to include, along with British, French, German, Italian, Russian and Spanish writers, texts by many writers from the European periphery, including Bulgaria, Norway, Poland, Portugal, Romania, Slovenia, Turkey and the Czech Republic. A second problem was the representation of major writers and even cultures, for whom we did not manage to find adequate translations. Since our main priority was to provide attractive readings for students, we decided to abstain from claims to representation and judge by the quality of the translated version rather than that of the original — keeping in mind that every masterpiece loses its value when it is read in an awkward translation.

Although the subject was taught in few schools last year, the anthology was very well received and we got some enthusiastic reports from instructors and students. Still, European literature poses to many instructors a major challenge, since on the one hand they have not been taught anything relevant at the University and, on the other, they have to teach <u>translated</u> texts from a wide variety of cultures, something which requires an entirely different methodology from that which serves the instruction of a national literature. So we have started a special research project, which aims to provide methodological support and material for the instruction of European literature at the secondary education. This project presently occupies six researchers, who organize extensive electronic files with theoretical, critical and literary texts which can be used in the context of the European literature class; this material will be at the disposal of teachers and students by the end of this year, through the Web Site of the Centre for the Greek Language (www.komvos.edu.gr), which will also furnish Greek Lyceums with material on several aspects of language teaching. I should also mention that we have joined a collective project along with colleagues from Britain, France, Germany, Italy and Spain, which is funded by the European Program CONNECT and aims to produce an integrated framework for the instruction of comparative literature in the secondary education across Europe.

The final project I will present began in 1994 and will hopefully be completed by the end of this year. Here we locate, collect and evaluate 19th and 20th-century translations of foreign literary texts, aiming at an extensive two-volume anthology of poetry and prose in Greek translation (I am responsible for the prose section and Professor Nassos Vayenas is responsible for the poetry section). We have gathered a large quantity of excellent texts, and are currently in the process of the final selection. What we are trying to produce is a work which on the one hand will reflect the history of Greek literary translation and on the other will challenge the traditional prejudice, which views translated literature as derivative or somehow insignificant compared to literature in the original.

Let me conclude by affirming our awareness that translation is the only available means for cultural communication, and that in Greece we need to work very hard in order to liberate ourselves from ethnocentric inhibitions which have traditionally restrained our cultural potential. I know that similar problems and views exist elsewhere, particularly in other countries of the European periphery. However, we must admit that at this stage we are still basically working in solitude, still trying to imagine the richer and more generous identity we have been deprived of for way too long.

Modern Greek Literature in Danish Translation

by
Rolf Hesse

Although it is not my field of study – which is language, especially lexicography - I'm going to present an overview of Danish translations of Modern Greek Literature. This could never have been done without support from Vibeke Espholm, Lars Nørgaard and Henrik Holmboe, for whose help I am very grateful. The result of this cooperation is a detailed bibliography.

The bibliography comprises not only books, but also short texts published in magazines and anthologies (sometimes found together with non fictional texts or with literary texts translated from other languages). Even though the list is hardly complete, I believe it to be representative enough to support the following observations:

The oldest Danish translation of a Modern Greek text found to date is from the year 1838: It is the novel «Ο εξόριστος του 1831» by Alexandros Soutsos, with the Danish title: "Den forviste fra 1831. En Roman fra Grækenlands nyeste Historie". It was translated from German by Arthur Conradsen. The Greek original was published in 1835.

Which books have been translated?

From 1838 to 1960, a period of over 120 years, only about 20 Modern Greek texts were translated into Danish, most of them not directly from Greek, but through Swedish, German or another language. From 1960 to 1999 there are at least 70 items, and many more if each single short story in anthologies is included.

From 1838 to 1960 almost only prose was translated: novels, short stories, folk tales - and τα Μυστήρια της Κεφαλονιάς by Laskaratos, a critical satirical book on manners and customs on the island of Kefalonia, translated in 1868. Even famous poets like Palamas and Drossinis are represented by prose texts. Poetry is represented in the 19th century only by 2 small books of folk songs. In 1960 we again get 'Græske folkesange', a selection of folk songs, translated by Ole Wahl Olsen. But the year 1960 and the name of Ole Wahl Olsen announce the beginning of a new era: from this year on direct translations from Greek of prose and poetry are published continuously, in the beginning almost exclusively by Ole Wahl Olsen. Thus a selection of Seferis' poems came out in 1963 and a selection of Elytis' poems in 1979, i.e. exactly in the years when these poets were awarded the Nobel prize. This was made possible by the fact that Ole Wahl Olsen had his drawers full of translations of the best Greek poets, more or less ready for publishing. During the 7 years of the dictatorship (1967-1974) he translated many anti-junta texts: e.g. Το λάθος "The Error" by Samarakis and a short story by Sotiris Patatzis. Also the famous "Z" by Vassilikos was translated, but this time by Karen Mathiasen who based her work on a French translation.

Ole Wahl Olsen's importance as a translator of Modern Greek literature can hardly be overestimated; he knew and knows personally a large number of poets and authors and he was the first to translate Antonis Samarakis (by now he has translated almost his complete work) and thus made him known outside Greece.

Only in about 1979 do the names of other translators begin to appear: Willy Gjerløv Pedersen translated the poet Giannis Kontós and has since translated a large number of modern poets: Dinos Christianopoulos, Tzeni Mastoraki, Antonis Fostieris and others. As for prose, we get a series of novels translated into Danish: Η αρραβωνιαστικιά του Αχιλλέα (Achilleas' forlovede) written by Alki Zei, Μεθυσμένα πολιτεία by Sotiris Patatzis (with the inappropriate, commercialized title: Primadonnaen), and Το ελληνικό φθινόπωρο της Εβα-Ανίτα Μπένγκτσον by Dimosthenis Kourtovik, Αστραδενή by Eugenia Fakinou. Several short stories have also been translated. Unfortunately there are still examples of translations through other languages: In a short story by Dimosthenis Voutyras, "Pararlama", from 1958, published in 1999 in a Danish anthology with the economic support of the EU, we find the following expression:

hans mor (...) gik med et kerchief.
("his mother wore a kerchief")

The following explanation is found in the notes at the end of the book:

> kerchief *(the English word, unknown in Danish)*: a headscarf, black or other colour, worn by old women or widows to cover their head.

The note makes it evident that the translation has been made from English, and that the translator believed the word *kerchief* to be Greek.

Which authors are translated?

Three recognized authors are represented by more than 4 titles each: Kazantzakis, Sotiris Patatzis and Antonis Samarakis. Kazantzakis does not surprise us: in the 1950's publishers were interested in this world known author, and as no Dane could be found with sufficient knowledge of Modern Greek, translations were made mainly via Swedish translations. In the case of Patatzis and Samarakis the explanation for their being translated is different: It was the translator's personal enthusiasm for their works, combined with a conviction, that the Danish reading public would like them. Samarakis in fact was a success.

A chronological view of the publishing years of authors translated more than twice gives the following picture:

Three texts by Kostis Palamas were translated between 1888 and 1936. At the beginning of the century we find Dimitrios Vikelas represented 4 times by short texts. In the 1950's there are 4 books of Kazantzakis, followed by 2 more in the 60's. Stratis Myrivilis puts in an appearance with 3 titles from 1958 to 1966, Antonis Samarakis with 7 from 1961 to 1988, Sotiris Patatzis with 5 titles between 1964 and 1994, and Vassilis Vassilikos with 4 titles from 1964 to 1999. Several poems by Kostas Varnalis, Georges Seferis and Odysseas Elytis have been translated in different reviews and anthologies during the last decades, but each of these authors is represented by only one book with their own works. Alki Zei is represented 3 times during the last 15 years. In addition, we find poems, songs and memories by Mikis Theodorakis (6 titles) and song texts written by Georges Marinos, a Greek living in Denmark (5 titles).

The translators

1960-1979 is the period of Ole Wahl Olsen, whose translations are almost always accompanied by illustrations, made by different excellent graphic illustrators. The result was a series of beautifully printed books. He is the translator of at least 40 published works.

After 1980 an increasing number of translators appears, resulting in a broader representation of Greek literature in Denmark. The personal enthusiasm of the translator is still of great importance, above all in the case of poetry. But the economic support of the EU and other funds and foundations play an increasingly important role together with the promotion by the Greek authors themselves, by the National Book Centre of Greece (see e.g. the new Greek Literary Review ITHACA) and now also by the Greek Ministry of Culture.

To sum up: today Danes can get acquainted with a great number of Greek authors. The excellent public library system in Denmark makes it easy for readers to get these translations free of charge. Many of the translations are competent, some indeed excellent, while others are more problematic. Furthermore we still need translations of some of the classics (e.g. Vizyinos and a complete Kavafis) as well as of new authors in the years to come. I hope that the bibliography will help readers to locate more easily the works they are looking for.

A Danish-Greek translation

Closing this short presentation I would like to "change direction" and mention a Danish text translated into Greek: In the old library of the school (Roskilde Katedralskole) where I teach, we found a small unbound booklet from 1860: Περί της Κατασκευής των ούτω καλουμένων Προδομών των Γιγάντων υπό του Μεγαλειοτάτου τε και φιλομούσου Βασιλέως της Δανίας Φριδερίκου του Z'. In Danish: "Om Bygningsmaaden af Oldtidens [saakaldte] Jættestuer, af hans Majestæt og museven Frederik den 7., Konge af Danmark." It was printed in Ermoupolis in Syros in 1860. The story of this translation falls outside my present subject. But I have the pleasure of presenting a copy of this book to the Danish Institute.

Note on Bibliography

Prior to the seminar 'Translators and Translations' at The Danish Institute at Athens in September 1999, Vibeke Espholm, Rolf Hesse and Henrik Holmboe decided to present a bibliography of Modern Greek Literature in Danish translation at the seminar.

The result is based upon several sources, i.a. a thorough examination of The Danish National Bibliography ("Dansk Bogfortegnelse") from 1841 to 1998.

The bibliographical material is presented in three separate booklets arranged in the following ways:
- according to year of publication
- alphabetically after translator's name
- alphabetically after author's name.

At the time of the seminar we were not aware of any other initiative to make public a bibliography similar to the one we were preparing, and neither to our knowledge were any of the participants.

In August 2000 it became known that Sysse Engberg was publishing a "Bibliography of Modern Greek literature translated into Danish" ("Bibliografi over moderne græsk litteratur oversat til dansk") on the Internet. You can find it at the webaddress http://www.ellinika.bot.ku.dk/bibliografi.htm.

Therefore, our booklets exist in only a few, privately distributed copies.

A copy is available both at The Danish Institute at Athens and at The Nordic Library at Athens.

Vibeke Espholm   Rolf Hesse   Henrik Holmboe

On Translating S. Kierkegaard's *Philosophical Fragments* into Greek

by
Sophia Scopetea

My initial purpose had been to discuss very briefly some problems that arise in relation to Kierkegaard's *Philosophical Fragments* and a possible translation into Greek.

The long process of deliberation was suddenly interrupted and the possibility turned into actuality: there does exist today a complete translation of *Fragments* into Greek - although not in such a way as to render a new attempt superfluous[1].

Philosophical Fragments can be placed, at first sight, on the philosophical level of Kierkegaard's work.

Let us imagine this space - or rather mode or aspect - as a factor of balance between the so called aesthetical (first part of *Either-Or* for example) and the religious works. Kierkegaard does not distinguish it himself either as philosophy or balance.

This is closer to wishful theory than textual fact: there is never pure philosophy in Kierkegaard. There are always interventions or admix-

---

[1] There is not one shadow of polemical intention in this remark and not the slightest doubt about the translator's integrity. That he translates from the French - which is clearly stated - is perfectly understandable, and there is no reason to doubt the reliability of his source. On the other hand, the danger of involuntary deviation from the original in this indirect type of translating is so obvious that it does not even need to be discussed. One could also disagree with some of the translator's solutions - as regards the title for instance - or his general attitude towards terminology, including Greek from the classical past (Kierkegaard, *Philosophica psichia*, translated by Costis Papagiorgis, Castaniotis Press, Athens 1998. A translation of *Sickness Unto Death* appeared one year later, in 1999, by the same translator and publishing house in Athens).

tures from both sides. The aesthetical factor is never entirely absent, and philosophical concepts or propositions tend to point beyond philosophy into the realm of religion (that is to say, Christian doctrine).

Key concepts such as the repetition, the moment, or despair are developed dialectically as it were for the sole purpose of being applied to theology.

There is a tendency to begin by translating terms or concepts first. I would not believe that terminological problems ever can be solved in a literary vacuum, nor that they can be settled once and for all and applied consistently from work to work. The dialectical pair actual-possible, from which I incidentally started in my first paragraph, would be a very good example. The consistency required for translating Kierkegaard or for that matter any other writer - even for scribbling a fragment of a sentence on a bit of paper is of a different order and cannot be either automatic or mechanical.

All terminological elements are directly influenced by their contextual surrounding, even the most solid concept can be affected and transformed. Style or mood or the writer's specific dialectical purposes or errands can also be decisive. What we thus observe in the original text must by all efforts be preserved in translation. A shift of words that might not occur in the original could turn out to be indispensable when you transfer into a different language.

This applies to all conceptual terms, philosophical or other, including those originating from Greek philosophy, an area that becomes highly relevant when it comes to translating into Greek.

One can distinguish the way in which those words are used in *The Repetition*, the deliberate play that forms their source. Think of the grand opening, with the Eleats stubbornly rejecting movement, refuted in the deed by the walking Diogenes, "as everybody knows", as every child in the land is supposed to be familiar with: a sentence, in the same joking mood, twisted out of Hegel[2].

---

[2] Hegel says nothing more than: "it is well known", Es ist bekannt (chapter on Zeno the Eleat in *The History of Philosophy*).
For the *Repetition* in English reference should be made to *Fear and Trembling / Repetition*, Edited and translated by Howard V. Hong and Edna H. Hong, Princeton U-

This first paragraph is a very crucial one for the whole of the book. It is a solemn declaration of the most sublime project, that of defining movement and the repetition (which ultimately becomes an issue of salvation or loss), triumphantly defeating both Germany and the Greeks at their own game. But the elevated project has to be carried out in a very prosaic manner, that is by childishly reiterating a journey to Berlin.

Some pages later in the same book Kierkegaard sums up Greek philosophical accomplishments, both real and imagined, where the towering concept turns out to be movement (kinesis).

Neither a joke nor a serious philosophical proposition: but simultaneously both. The Greeks are not praised for their own sake (as indeed nobody would argue that they should), but, as very often in the past, they are used as scales; in this particular case, in order to weigh Hegel and his concepts ("Aufhebung" in particular, this proud convergence of elevation-and-cancelling) and find them wanting.

The problem a Greek translator would have to solve in this case is not so much terminological accuracy - it does not present insurmountable problems anyway[3]. It is much more urgent to convey the tone, this jest-in-earnest, something that Howard Hong[4], joking himself, defined as "*j*esture".

In literature no exact translation is possible, even with the most ideal presuppositions. (It would suffice to think about proper names, that do not always have to be exotic. Think for instance of the Modern Greek name: Athanassios / Thanassis, not at all uncommon. In a translation it would usually be transliterated; but what if the author in a particular instance used it in such a precise way as to awake associations of death or immortality? Or, to make for a moment a more subtle thought: what of

---

niversity Press 1983. My own tranlation (*He Epanalipsi*) appeared in Athens in 1977 (Papazissis Publisher).

[3] Depending of course on the optimism of the observer. Nothing (Intet in Danish) can amount either to the everyday τίποτα, not-one-thing, or μηδέν, which is null but always, through the same language practice, inextricably associated with the circle of a zero.

[4] Orally in a lecture given in Copenhagen in the early eighties, if memory does not fail me.

the title name *Lambros*, giving a hint of illumination to an otherwise demonic character, by the poet Dionysios Solomos. Similar cases can be imagined in any other language.) Between languages, even those connected to each other by the most intimate bonds, there is always a transformation taking place going far beyond the mere converting of words, even when it is most accurate. On the other hand, bearing firmly those impossibilities in mind, translating is a task that certainly can be accomplished, without necessarily betraying the original.

You could be tempted to diverge on the importance of some translated texts through time, the vicissitudes that have bestowed on some of them a character that makes the distinction between original and derivative text of minor importance, obliterating sources, or making us forget origin or simple historical facts. Let it suffice to mention the Greek Old Testament (The Septuagint), translated from the Hebrew - not always accurately, so at least argue qualified scholars.

On a more human level, when the first sentence of Wittgenstein's *Tractatus logico-philosophicus* ("Die Welt ist Alles, was der Fall ist", inconceivable outside German) has been translated into English, of all languages, and when the same philosopher has been able to conduct his thinking in two languages, one of them always remaining foreign even though not unknown: everything becomes suddenly more than translatable, and the issue of fidelity is transformed.

It should not be forgotten that Kierkegaard was very slow in attracting attention outside the Scandinavian countries. So there actually does not exist a translation that would genuinely convey the flavour of the 19th century with its heavy romantic inheritance. With the exception of some parentheses in the past (in Germany *The Book of the Judge* and a small number of subsequent disparate publications[5]; in France, translations of some religious writings within protestant circles, more or less marginal)[6], it is only since the 30's that Kierkegaard is systematically translat-

---

[5] Kafka had nevertheless read both *The Book of the Judge*, which is a selection from Kierkegaard's Journals, and *Either-Or*, and was deeply impressed; see for example his journal entry for August 21, 1913.

[6] Cf. Peter Kemp, "Le précurseur de Henrik Ibsen", Quelques aspects de la découverte de Kierkegaard en France, *Les Études philosophiques*, no. 2, 1979, pp. 139-150.

ed into German, French or English (the latter mostly in the United States).

A consequence of this delay is that translated Kierkegaard has essentially become a writer of the 20th century. In other words, to take the inevitable next step, he can be read - and legitimately so - as a writer who presupposes Modernist experimentations.

When it comes to translating into Greek, Kierkegaard's deliberate incompatibilities can perfectly well be rendered by allowing a mixture of styles and idioms such as have been practised by Kavafis, Papadiamantis or the Surrealists - upon the condition of not doing it mechanically or as an imitation of any particular author. These are styles[7] which have been incorporated into the written language, helping to surpass the schism (much exaggerated anyway) between vernacular and "pure" Greek.

Very often in Kierkegaard the Greek terms appear directly in Greek. This is extraordinary, but in no way a unique case, although one could remark that Greek in this direct sense does not occur in Nietzsche who was after all by education a genuine Classical scholar.

In that case the Greek translator leaves the classical terms as they are, distinguishing them only by typography, adding explanations when necessary. (*The Concept of Irony* is a different case, being the only book in which Kierkegaard quotes so extensively in both Greek and German.) The effect is certainly not the same. Though the precise effect they produced, stylistically, at the time and place of their publication, even supposing that all contemporary readers were familiar with the language foreign to the text, is extremely difficult to evaluate.

Of all foreign languages German is supposed to be the nearest to Danish, outside Scandinavia (where a translation would be superfluous, one might argue, although there have been instances, at least into Swedish). This is perfectly true, when one thinks of the cultural ties between Denmark and Germany in the past, and Kierkegaard's intimate familiarity

---

[7] One could incidentally remark that punctuation is included in style, and this means that the argument against retaining Kierkegaard's lengthy sentences is not beyond refutation. There is neither uniformity nor predictability anyway. The author lets very often a sudden question, a brief poignant utterance, or other syncopating elements intercept the flow of even the most strenuous clause.

with both German literature and philosophy[8]. But the same German becomes the most distant when Kierkegaard uses it against the grain to produce ironic effects within his own Danish text.

This effect is not entirely lost in Greek. German can convey in popular consciousness the tone of an all too extreme seriousness or even (after the experiences of the last war) an all-encompassing threat. According to current convention it has to be left untranslated[9] - one should remember that Kierkegaard's German includes Shakespeare[10]. But even with the similarities or analogies we have noted, the discontinuity produced by German in the Greek text is certainly more marked.

Philosophical Fragments and its translation problems are of a different order than those of *Repetition*. The jest-in-earnest is finished. Greek becomes very prominent, but not necessarily in terms of language. It is no longer a question of just alluding to Socrates, or even treating him by a series of theses, as in the dissertation on Irony. He is placed on the scene from the outset. The reference is to him personally, but no reference to Socrates can be achieved in a literary void, one has to pass through Plato. There have to be Platonic reminiscences, especially so if the translation is going to be into Greek.

Reminiscence means in this case that you have to evoke a Platonic landscape. This is achieved by means of words (which do not have to be Plato's own), in a learned (Kierkegaard, even if he at times aimed at it, cannot be considered as a popular writer), though certainly noterudite

---

[8] This is much envied by translators into English, as for instance Walter Lowrie, struggling with such terms as Bestemmelse (Bestimmung, later translated as "qualification") or Tvivl/Fortvivlelse (Zweifel/Verzweiflung, in English only doubt and despair; the Greek association for the latter term is ἀπελπισία [apelpisia], loss of hope).

[9] A natural subject for a footnote, although the space of footnotes should by no means be misused, unnecessarily enhanced or, still worse, practised as a subterfuge. I would still insist on that, even after having multiplied a slender *Repetition* to the size of some 500 pages: the notes were accompanied by a commentary and the reader in no way urged or even encouraged to read them anyway. A translator should never forget that the battle has to be fought within the text itself.

[10] He always quoted from the Tieck and Schlegel translation, which already by his time had acquired the status of a classic (a new instance of a translation imperceptibly being converted into original text, as discussed above).

manner. Regardless how, the translation into Greek has to be done having Plato in mind. I cannot become more precise on this point, certainly not for the sake of mystification, only for the simple reason that I have not yet begun translating. Pursuing a path of preliminary deliberations is a long way from actually working on a book, and it is only within work that solutions arise.

Socrates in *Fragments* is not presented for his own sake. He has to function as a measure, or a middle term, between humanity and the divine. He has to prove the superior status of Christianity, and at the same time the inadequacy of current, i.e. German, speculative philosophy (as Kierkegaard resumes in his Conclusion).

The difficulty of the book is that Christianity is never mentioned by name, it is constructed philosophically as if it were a pure experiment. This leaves *Repetition* far behind, adding at the same time a new dimension of, depending on the point of view, either a higher dialectical fusion or an incompatibility, i.e. an attitude which can be dogmatical in the extreme, while it unfolds within a thoroughly experimental setting.

Whether Kierkegaard's terminological ambiguity is immediately retrievable in Greek I would not answer as yet. It is something you cannot avoid struggling with, as it appears already on the title page, through terms as portent as belief/faith and happiness/salvation (in Danish conveyed deliberately by one word, Tro and Salighed respectively). I would not risk suggesting any answer as to the ideal solution. But as a general principle I would strongly argue that any equivocal expression in the original must retain its character also in the translated text. Needless to say, not at the cost of creating hybrid constructions or paper words[11].

Those are apparently difficulties of not quite the same kind but of equal intensity to that of translating the strophe on love-in-recollection by the poet P.M. Møller in the *Repetition*.

Translating *Philosophical Fragments* is also connected with more modest or more specific problems. The title for instance.

The term Fragment should be avoided, it is too intimately connected

---

[11] The construct "l'être-là" invented by French translators of Dasein is a very good example of what I have in mind.

with either the involuntary piece or shred of text, the Presocratics, or the deliberate Romantic practice.

Instead of the original subtitle ("A Bit of Philosophy") Papagiorgis[12] has chosen to transfer the epigraph of *Concluding Unscientific Postscript*, from the Platonic *Hippias Major* 304a in Plato's words (κνήσματα καὶ περιτμήματα) those miserable bits and scraps, which have become almost completely opaque in Modern Greek. The expression is not uncongenial and the connection between the two units, Kierkegaard's title and the Platonic words, is not at all irrelevant. It remains dubious though from the point of view of philology, which is a discipline very much congenial to translating.

The name Johannes Climacus, Kierkegaard's pseudonym-in-chief (he is the supposed author of the *Fragments*, while Kierkegaard presents himself as the mere editor on the title page), must retain its Latin form and not be transliterated back into Greek, in order to distinguish from the original John of Climax, who among other things also was an author of texts pertaining to theology.

On the other hand we have the Aristotelian terminology: possible-actual-necessary (here principally used for defending human and divine freedom), in the dialectical treatment of which Kierkegaard is again addressing Hegel. Ontology becomes ethics, in the perspective of Christian dogmatics, and unfolds in a dialectical development of proving and refuting freedom, human and divine.

The Greek translator can do nothing more than recur to Aristotle's unmediated terms. One cannot change the fact of the reversal that has taken place, it is impossible to do more than comment on it.

The issue of freedom over against the necessity of predestination has never plagued the ancient (or for that matter the subsequent) Greeks in quite the same way. It is a Christian predicament, if it absolutely must be seen in terms of a predicament.

---

[12] See above n. 1.

Achilleus Paraschos and Two Danish Folk Songs

by
Lars Nørgaard

Θα ήταν αφέλεια να πιστεύουμε πως θα ήταν δυνατό να προσεχτεί από ξένους σαν αντικείμενο μελέτης η ρομαντική περίπτωση της Ελλάδας.
Ανδρέας Καραντώνης (1981)

Αλλ' όμως πόσα δεν λαλούν εις την ψυχήν οι τάφοι;
Αχ. Παράσχος, Ο άγνωστος ποιητής (1863)

In the last two decades or so a remarkable tendency in Modern Greek literary criticism has been the study and re-evaluation of the so-called first Athenian School of poets and prose writers. This term is one of several being used to designate the representatives of the romantic literary movement in 19th century Greece, two generations of writers conventionally placed in the 50 years between 1830 and 1880, with its centre the capital of Greece and as such, in the history of Modern Greek literature, opposed to the contemporary romantics on the Ionian Islands.

There are various reasons for the renewed interest in this period and its literary products. The most obvious, but not the only one, is the generally changing attitude to the archaizing language used by these poets to express their romantic sentiments.

So far, it has primarily been the prose tradition of the Athenian School that has received the attention of scholars, and it has been combined and extended with studies on the local reception and transmission of the great European romantic models, e.g. on Walter Scott and his influence on Greek romantics, and translations as well as methods and principles of translation have been discussed. The Athenian romantic poetry of the same period may well be next in line.

The subject of the following remarks falls within this area, as I wish to present and discuss the translations of two Danish folk songs, made by the foremost romantic poet, Achilleus Paraschos. The translations - or *imitations* as they were called by Paraschos[1] - were both published in Athenian literary reviews within the space of about ten years, the first in 1865, the second in 1876. Both were after substantial revision included in the famous 1881-edition of Paraschos' poems. They were not the first Danish literary texts to be translated or in other ways communicated to Greece or the Greek speaking area, but they were among the first of a group of translations that may be said to owe their existence to a broader Greek interest in Danish culture. This interest was of course closely connected to the change of regime in 1863.

Danish literature in Greece around 1863

In the following, and as a background to my discussion of the translations of the two ballads, I shall give a short survey of the fate of Danish literature in Greece around 1863 in which the translations of Paraschos are set. Necessarily, the survey will have a preliminary character: we do not possess a complete catalogue of translations made into Greek in the 19th century, which means that many translations may hide for instance in the periodical literature of the period[2].

In spite of this, it seems to be a safe conclusion that before 1863 knowledge of Danish literature was almost non existent in the Greek area. Around 1863 the conditions favoured an interest in Danish literature

---

[1] Αχιλλέως Παράσχου *Ποιήματα* Α΄, Ανδρέας Κορομηλάς εκδότης. Εν Αθήναις - Εν Κωνσταντινουπόλει, 1881, 311- 318. Paraschos' notes here indicate that the first translation was originally made in 1863, the second in 1873 (op. cit., 314 and 318). The changes made by Paraschos from the versions of the reviews to the 1881-edition are registered in my Appendices below.

[2] Σοφία Ντενίση, *Μεταφράσεις μυθιστορημάτων και διηγημάτων 1830-1880. Εισαγωγική μελέτη και καταγραφή*, Αθήνα (Περίπλους) 1995 does not cover the literary reviews of the time, see however p. 11 on the existing instrumenta. A complete bibliography of 19th cent. translations into Greek has been announced by K. G. Kasines, who is the author of several studies in this area of research, collected now in Κ. Γ. Κασίνης, *Διασταυρώσεις. Μελέτες για τον ΙΥ΄ και Κ΄ αι.*, Αθήνα 1998.

with the purpose of informing the Greek reading audience about the cultural background of the new royal house. With one or two exceptions translations were not made from Danish, but predominantly from French. The translators were not in every case literary writers, but could be critics or persons who had superficial contact with Denmark or the royal house and wished to demonstrate that. Several of these translations were of a poor quality, made by persons in a more or less marginal position in Greek cultural life. The case of Paraschos translating two of the most famous ballads of Danish folk poetry has none of these characteristics: it was made by the foremost romantic writer of the period and we are allowed to surmise that any new product from this gifted poet would get attention among his wide Greek circle of readers, stretching far beyond the national territory of Greece[3].

In many cases the translations of Danish literature into Modern Greek have been the result of personal connections or specific preferences, but around 1863 the situation is somewhat different. After more than 40 years of constitutional fights the arrival of the young king raised the hope of political stability. In this context, the history and political traditions of the native country of the Greek king were extolled as being able to contribute to the stabilisation of the Greek political system. This was reflected in the publications of the period. In newspapers and books Denmark - called either Δανιμαρκία or Δανία - was presented as the stabile monarchy with hundreds of years' democratic tradition that was supposed to be transmitted and continued in Greece in the person of the young monarch.

Many aspects of Danish history and culture were at the same time introduced in Greece. So, in the highly esteemed review *Pandora* the critic Konstantinos Pop wrote in 1863 an article entitled 'Danish Philology' and with the following words he proposes to present specimens of Danish literature in the *Pandora*:

"I shall restrain myself to communicating to the readers of this distinguished review some Danish short stories, turned into Greek from the French translation by the well-known French scholar Xavier Marmier.

---

[3] Of course the expression "wide" is relative as percentages of illiteracy were high, cf. Sophia Denissi, The image of Britain in *Pandora*, Kampos No. 5, 1997, 25.

The translator found these stories in two anthologies, published in Copenhagen in 1853 with the title "Short Stories, New and Old" ("Noveller, nye og gamle"), and "New Short Stories" ("Nye Fortællinger"), attributed to Mr L. Heiberg, one of the most ingenuous and popular authors and playwriters, on the same rank as the equally famous writers Oehlenschläger, Andersen, Ingemann, Hauch, Blicher, as well as the poets Paludan-Møller and Winther"[4].

In the same number of *Pandora* Pop publishes a translation of a short story by the to-day seldom read Mrs Gyllembourg, called 'The Small Karen' ('Η μικρά Καρίνα') and states as his purpose to publish translations of two other stories from the collections in the following issues of the *Pandora* - a promise, however, he did not fulfil. The stories were, in the words of Pop, remarkable because of their "ethical contents", besides being "charming and interesting"[5].

Another typical example to show that what was translated was not - as we see it today - in every case representative of Danish literature or of the writer in question, but sometimes due to casuality and/or to the preferences of the translator, is the translation of the national poet Steen Steensen Blicher, whose minor novel 'Poor Louis' was translated from the French and published by Marinos Papadopoulos-Vretos in his *National Yearbook of 1865*. The translator Papadopoulos-Vretos, diplomate

---

[4] Op. cit., 436. I have corrected the spelling of several of the authors mentioned by Pop (and Marmier). The exact meaning of the Greek text is in some places dubious, and therefore rendered here: "... αρκούμαι να μεταδώσω τοις αναγνώσταις του αξιολόγου υμών περιοδικού συγγράμματος διηγήματά τινα Δανικά, εξελληνίζων αυτά εκ της Γαλλικής μεταφράσεως του γνωστού Γάλλου λογίου Xavier Marmier. Τα διηγήματα ταύτα απήνθισεν ο μεταφραστής εκ δύο συλλογών, εκδοθεισών εν Κοπεγχάγη το 1853 και επιγραφόμενα 'Διηγήματα νέα και παλαιά' (δανιστί, Noveller, gamle og nye) και 'Νέα διηγήματα' (Nye Fortaellinger), αποδιδόμενα δε εις τον Κ. Λ. Εϊβέργον (L. Heiberg), ένα των αφελεστέρων και δημοτικωτέρων συγγραφέων και δραματοποιών της Δανίας, καταττόμενον μετά των εξίσου περιφανών λογογράφων Oehlenschläger, Andersen, Ingemann, Hauch, Blicher, και των ποιητών Paludan-Møller και Winther".

[5] Mrs Gyllembourg's 'Den lille Karen' was originally published in *Kjøbenhavns flyvende Post* in 1830, the Greek translation 'Η μικρά Καρίνα' in *Πανδώρα* 15, 1864-65. The stories were said by Pop to be "ου μόνον πλήρη χάριτος και διαφέροντος, αλλ' όπερ και το κάλλιστον, ηθικώτατα", op. cit., 436.

and publisher from an Ionian family of high intellectual standing and social position, had been in Denmark together with the Greek election committee in spring 1863, where he among others met the Danish scholar Jean Pio, with whom he shared the interest in the Danish poet[6].

However, the predominant figure was of course H. C. Andersen. As we saw, he is mentioned in the *Pandora* article, but apart from that, the first presentation seems to have been that of the review *Chrysallis* in 1864 with the title 'Ιωάννης Ανδερσεν'[7]. This article does not exhibit any originality (nor does it claim any) and does not demonstrate any firsthand knowledge of the poet's work. The description of the poet's career stops around 1845, he is extolled as a poet with a reference to the poem 'The Dying Child' ('Det døende Barn', in Greek 'Το θνήσκον τέκνον') and as a novelist. There is no mention of the fairytales. It is an anonymous article of encyclopaedic character, possibly translated from French by one of the editors of the *Chrysallis*, who may have found the French text in the *Revue des deux mondes* or the *Revue de Paris*. It was outdated when it was presented in Greece and that is was translated mechanically from its model is shown by the remarkable fact that Andersen's relations to Greece, described in *The Bazar of a Poet* (*En Digters Bazar*, publ. 1842, in Greek *Η αγορά του ποιητού*) is only mentioned passingly.

The first original work of Andersen to be translated - and the introduction in Greece of his fairytales - was the 'The Nightingale', published in a translation into mixed learned and vernacular Greek by the Danish neohellenist Jean Pio, who in 1864-65 was studying Modern Greek language in Greece. It appeared in the newspaper *Eunomia*, owned and edited by the

---

[6] Blicher's 'Stakkels Ludvig' (originally publ. in *Nordlyset* 1827) was published with the title 'Ο ταλαίπωρος Λουδοβίκος' in *Εθνικόν ημερολόγιον του έτους 1865* ('Ετος Ε'), εκδοθέν υπό Μαρίνου Παπαδοπούλου-Βρετού. On the French translation, see Poul Skadhauge, Blicher på fremmede sprog, in: *Omkring Blicher* 1974, 52-53. The copy of the 1863 almanac in the possession of the Gennadeios Library, Athens, belonged originally to Jean Pio and, as a handwritten note shows, was donated to him by Papadopoulos-Vretos himself in Copenhagen, June 1863. On this, see Lars Nørgaard, O Jean Pio και οι απαρχές των νεοελληνικών σπουδών στη Δανία, *Πόρφυρας* 78, 1996, 380.

[7] 'Ιωάννης Ανδερσεν', *Χρυσαλλίς* Β', 1864, 665-668. The French original may have been written by Xavier Marmier, see below.

diplomate-publisher Alexandros Rizos Rangavis. As in the case of Pop, more translations were announced, but never published. Among the reasons for the publication the editor mentions the charm and naivity of the tale[8]. The next step in the Greek reception of Andersen was the adaptation by the social and moral reformator from Cefalonia Andreas Laskaratos of the famous 'History of a Mother', based on a translation by Jean Pio and published by Laskaratos in his family magazine *The Lamp*[9]. While the translation of Pio may be said to render the original reliably, Laskaratos changed the contents radically in order to make it serve the ideological purposes of his review. As he stated in a letter to Pio commenting on the translation: "the publication of moral folktales can contribute to the resurrection of the Orient"[10]. He starts in Greece the tradition of Andersen-*imitations*, as opposed to translations, often - but not in the case of Laskaratos- without any indication of the original. Until 1875 several translations of fairytales were published, e.g. the 'History of a Coin' by Demetrios Vikelas, who was also a friend of Pio, in the *Estia*[11], and 'The Shadow' in the *National Library* of Matarangas[12]. The first collection of Andersen's tales was published by Vikelas in 1873[13].

---

[8] 'Το αηδόνι', *Ευνομία* 1865, φυλλ. 232, 233 and 235. The translation of the fairytale (the original 'Nattergalen' publ. 1843 in the collection *Nye Eventyr*) was made in spring 1865 when Pio was working in Athens on Greek popular literature, see Lars Nørgaard, op. cit., 375-392.

[9] 'Μητρική αγάπη', *Ο λύχνος*, αριθμ. 44, 30 Απριλίου 1868 ν.ε. (= Άπαντα Ανδρέα Λασκαράτου, επιμ. Α. Παπαγεωργίου και Αντ. Μοσχοβάκη, τομ. Γ', Αθήνα 1959, 413-415), cf. Lars Nørgaard, op. cit. 382-83 and 389. Andersen's fairytale 'Historien om en Moder' was originally published in the collection *Nye Eventyr* II, 1848.

[10] The letter dated 24 January 1867 was published in Σ. Β. Κουγέας, Δύο γράμματα του Λασκαράτου - Από την ελληνικήν αλληλογραφίαν του Δανού φιλολόγου Πίο, *Νέα Εστία* 27, 1940, 4-9.

[11] 'Ιστορία μιας δραχμής', *Εστία* 1871, 189-191. The Danish original 'Sølvskillingen' was published 1861.

[12] 'Η σκιά. Κατά το Δανικόν του Anderson' [!], *Εθνική βιβλιοθήκη* (του Νικολάου Ματαράγκα). Έτος έβδομον, 1872-1873, 102-108. The translator was I.K. (probably Ιωάννης Καμπούρογλους, see Α. Σαχίνης, *Συμβολή στην ιστορία της Πανδώρας και των παλιών περιοδικών*, Αθήνα 1964, 103). The Danish original 'Skyggen' was published 1847.

[13] *Παραμύθια δανικά εκ του Άνδερσεν. Μεταφρασθέντα υπό Δ. Βικέλα χάριν των*

The imitations of Paraschos

By common consent, the poet Achilleus Paraschos was the most illiterate of the Athenian romantics[14]. In fact, this was already the opinion of his contemporaries, so that when the politician and man of letters Timoleon Philemon after the death of Paraschos, at a commemorative meeting (Ημερίς) dedicated to the poet, touched the subject he subtly turned what might seem a deficiency into a virtue by stating that the originality of Paraschos' poetry was exactly due to his ignorance of foreign languages[15].

Many contemporary and later critics commented on this to the same effect. Palamas, for one, was to give the argument a further twist stating that, despite this ignorance on the part of Paraschos, he was by the mere power of his poetic intuition connected with the French and British romantics[16].

ανεψίων του. Εν Λειψία 1873. The recent bibliography of K. Ntelopoulos does not include fairytales published in reviews (Κυρ. Ντελόπουλος, *Παιδικά και νεανικά βιβλία του 19ου αιώνα*, Αθήνα 1995). For some recent interesting conclusions on Andersen in Greece, see Μαριάνθη Καπλάνογλου, *Ελληνική λαϊκή παράδοση. Τα παραμύθια στα περιοδικά για παιδιά και νέους (1836-1922)*, Αθήνα 1998, 177-211.

[14] Γλ. Πρωτοπαπά-Μπουμπουλίδου, *Η αθηναϊκή σχολή*, Ιωάννινα 1976, 34.

[15] "Όχι ολίγοι είναι οι έχοντες την γνώμην, ότι ο Αχ. Παράσχος θα ανεδεικνύετο μεγαλύτερος, εάν εγνώριζε ξένας γλώσσας και ηδύνατο να κατέχη τα ξένας ποιήσεις εις τας γλώσσας όπου αύται συνετέθησαν. Και όμως, το ιδιάζον της ποιήσεώς του ο Αχ. Παράσχος το οφείλει εις την άγνοιαν των ξένων φιλολογιών. Εάν εγνώριζε ξένας γλώσσας, εφ' όσον είχε τάσιν εις το απαύστως αναγινώσκειν, θα τας εγνώριζε τόσον καλώς, ώστε θα επέδρων επ' αυτού αι ιδέαι και αι μορφαί των ξένων ποιητών. Και ο Παράσχος τότε θα έχανε τον κύριον χαρακτήρα της αμιγούς εμπνεύσεως, η οποία τον διέκρινεν εις το έργον του, και δεν θα εδικαιούτο του τίτλου, τον οποίον ο ίδιος εξαιρετικώς κατέκτησε, να θεωρείται δημιούργημα αμιγές και καθαρόν της Νέας Ελλάδος, προαχθέν και αναπτυχθέν, χωρίς την άμεσον επίδρασιν της ξένης φιλολογίας. Διότι όσα εκ των έργων της ανέγνωσεν εις μεταφράσεις εις την νεοελληνικήν γλώσσαν ελάχιστα επέδρασεν επί του πνεύματός του. Ιδού διατί, υπό την έποψιν αυτήν, εγένετο πράγματι, Εθνικός Ποιητής" ('Αντί προλόγου' in: Αχιλλέως Παράσχου *Ανέκδοτα ποιήματα*, Αθήνησι 1904, Τομ. Α', κβ').

[16] "Με μόνον την δύναμιν της ποιητικής του intuition συνδέετο μ' εκείνας (δηλ. τας

Be that as it may, in the final part of the first volume of the 1881- edition of Paraschos' collected poems, dedicated to Queen Olga, we find a section entitled *Translations* (Μεταφράσεις). These include, among others, translations of a part of Byron's *Childe Harold* (Σιλδ-Αρόλδ), as well as specimens of Scandinavian literature: 'The Smile, after Frederika Bremer. Imitation' ('Το μειδίαμα. Κατά την Φρειδερίκην Βρέμερ. Μίμησις'), 'Hopelessness, after the Finnish' ('Απελπισία. Κατά το Φιλλανδικόν'), 'Desire, after the Finnish' ('Πόθος. Κατά το Φιλλανδικόν'), and finally two poems described in the subtitle as 'Imitation after the Danish', ('Κατά το Δανικόν. Μίμησις')[17]. The first is entitled 'The Dead Knight' ('Ο νεκρός ιππότης') and the second 'A Mother's Return' ('Μητρός επάνοδος')[18]. They are Greek versions of two af the most famous Danish folk songs: 'Aage and Else' and 'The Return of the Dead'[19]. They belong to the category called *Magic ballads* (*Trylleviser*), more precisely to the group of *Ghost songs*, *Gengangerviser*, that is ballads relating the temporary resurrection of the dead and their interference with matters and persons of the living world. The first tells the story of the dead lover, who by the sorrow of his widowed wife is called upon to leave his grave to meet her. When he is forced to leave her in the morning, she follows him against his will and he only succeeds to slip into the grave by distracting her attention. One month after she dies from sorrow and they are united in the grave. The

---

royautés littéraires των Γάλλων), κ' ενεφανίζετο, εις τας ευτυχεστέρας του στιγμάς, και θυρωνικός και λαμαρτινικός ποιητής, τύπος νεοέλληνος ρωμαντικού, καθυστερεμένου κάπως" (Κ. Παλαμάς, Άπαντα, τόμ. 12, 18).

[17] The term mimisis (μίμησις or κατά μίμησιν) or imitation, against metaphrasis/paraphrasis, is not consequently used in the subtitles of the translations of Paraschos. It was a common label among the romantics to designate the relationship of a translation to the original, see e.g. P.D. Mastrodimitris, Οι μεταφράσεις του Καρασούτσα, *Ο ερανιστής* 10 (1972-73), 135 on Karasoutsas and Lafontaine. At the time it seems to be used to acknowledge another poet's intellectual property right to the work which was imitated or emulated. In our case it makes the imitation a pastiche.

[18] *Ποιήματα* A, 311- 318.

[19] The Danish titles are 'Aage og Else' and 'Den Dødes Igjenkomst'. They are now in the classic registration of *Danmarks gamle Folkeviser* (DgF) no. 90 as "Fæstemanden i Graven" and no. 89 as "Moderen under Mulde".

second relates the story of the dead mother who, moved by the lament of her orphan children tormented by their wicked stepmother, rises and by her appearance scares the stepmother and her weak husband to change their behaviour towards the children. The theme in both ballads is love surmounting even death.

At first sight, the mere existence of translations may seem surprising, given the fact that the translator was supposed to be illiterate. Secondly, the subject folk poetry may seem an unusual choice for an Athenian romantic. This raises several questions, among which the most obvious are: if the poet did not know any foreign language, how was he able to translate Danish folk ballads? Did he have an already translated version before him or if not, how were the contents conveyed to him and by whom? And finally, was the poetry of Paraschos by any chance influenced by the foreign models? In what follows I wish to discuss some of these issues[20].

As indicated after the texts of the translations in 1881, Paraschos composed his translation of 'The Dead Knight' in 1863, the year of the accession of the new king, while 'A Mother's Return' was composed in 1873. Furthermore, as already stated, the Danish ballads were published originally in Athenian literary reviews: 'The Dead Knight' came out in the before mentioned *Chrysallis* in 1865[21]. The poem was dedicated to Maria, the femme-fatale of Paraschos' early years.

'A Mother's Return' was published originally in the review *Byron* in 1876 with the subtitle 'After the Danish of Andersen' ('Κατά το Δανικόν του Andersen')[22]. As it will be clear from the collations, I have made in the Appendices, the texts were changed in various ways before they were incorporated in their final form in the first volume of the 1881-edition, which besides the translations includes the epics. The dedication to Maria in 'The Dead Knight' was thus left out as the love affair, a piece of gossip in the Athens of those years, had ended long a-

---

[20] The reader is referred to the synoptic versions of the ballads in the appendices. The citations from the texts of Paraschos is where nothing else is indicated from the 1881-edition.
[21] *Χρυσαλλίς* Γ', 1865, 653.
[22] *Βύρων* Β', 1876, 117-119.

go. Furthermore, in 1881 Paraschos seems, by himself or by the help of others, to have realised that what he imitated was not a poem by the great Danish story teller, although the subject, that of motherly love, was dear to Andersen both in poems and fairytales, and had being introduced in Greek literature by Andreas Laskaratos in 1868. The ascription shows lack of knowledge of Andersen's work, but may also suggest a distance between Paraschos and the original text. A more malicious interpretation would of course be that Paraschos in spite of his knowledge to the contrary attributed the poem to Andersen because he expected the name of the famous Dane to enhance wider public interest in the translation.

Where did Paraschos find the Danish folk songs?

As it is most unlikely that Paraschos had any knowledge of the Danish originals, the basis for his imitations should be sought in the translations of Danish folk songs and collections of folk songs available at his time. English and German translations did indeed exist, but given the fact that the Greek romantics took their models and inspiration from the French romantic movement, the probable source should be found there[23].

In his book *Chants populaires du Nord* (Paris 1842) Xavier Marmier, who has been mentioned in the precedent pages, presented specimens of Danish literature and among these also folk poetry, although he had no high opinion of its aesthetic values. Here we find translations of the two ballads that were imitated by Paraschos[24]. Marmier, for his part, found the Danish text in a collection of songs published in 1812 by three of the leading members of the early romantic movement in Denmark[25]. A comparison between the openings lines of the two ballads in the versions of

---

[23] On existing translations, see Erik Dal, Oversættelser af nordiske folkeviser, *Samlet og spredt om folkeviser*, Odense 1976, 9-29. On the French inspiration, see K. Th. Dimaras, Η ιδεολογική υποδομή του νέου ελληνικού κράτους, *Ελληνικός ρομαντισμός*, Αθήνα 1982, 352-53.

[24] *Chants populaires du Nord*, Paris 1842, 109-11 ('Le retour d'une mère'), 134-35 ('Aage et Else').

[25] *Udvalgte Danske Viser fra Middelalderen efter A.S. Vedel og Peder Syvs trykte Udgaver og efter haandskrevne Samlinger* udgivne paa ny af Abrahamson, Nyerup og Rahbek I, Kjøbenhavn 1812, 205-9 ('Den Dødes Igjenkomst') and 210-14 ('Aage og Else').

Marmier and of the Danish text should prove the point and at the same time show some typical solutions of Marmier to the problems of rendering the exotic text to a French public:

AAGE OG ELSE (1812)
Det var Ridder Herr Aage,
han red sig under Ø,
Fæsted han Jomfru Elselille,
hun var saa væn en Mø

Fæsted han Jomfru Elselille
　　Alt med saa meget Guld
Maanedsdagen derefter
　　laae han i sorten Muld

DEN DØDES IGJENKOMST (1812)
Svend Dyring han rider sig op under Ø,
　　Var jeg selver ung.
Der fæsted han sig saa væn en Mø,
Favre Ord fryde saa mangt et Hjerte.

Tilsammen vare de udi syv Aar,
　　Var jeg selver ung.
Sex Børn de tilsammen faaer,
Favre Ord fryde saa mangt et Hjerte.

AAGE ET ELSE (MARMIER, 1842)
Le chevalier Aage s'en va dans une île,
et se fiance avec Else, la belle jeune fille.
Il se fiance richement avec Else, la belle,
Un mois après, il était enseveli dans la tombe noir.

LE RETOUR D'UNE MÈRE (MARMIER, 1842)
Dyring s'en va dans une île et épouse une belle jeune fille. Ils vécurent ensemble sept ans et eurent six enfants.

Marmier gives an almost word-to-word prose translation of the Danish ballads without rhymes and refrains. He omits only what he did not understand or considered too exotic. As an example may be mentioned the first 2 lines of verse 5 of 'The Dead Knight', which run in the Danish original:
　　Han klapped paa Døren med Kiste,
　　　　Fordi han havde ej Skind[26].
　　He knocked on the door with the coffin,
　　　　because he had no cloak.
　This refers to the habit of knocking on a door with the sword on one's

---

[26] *Udvalgte Danske Viser..*, 211.

cloak ("Skind") and gave no meaning to Marmier, who omitted the line.

Marmier added nothing to the Danish model and his text is almost totally covered by the imitation of Paraschos, more so in the final versions of 1881 than in the earlier review versions. In the remaining part containing Paraschos' own contributions, there is no indication whatsoever that he should have had any knowledge of the Danish text beyond the French translation. From a philological point of view, a comparison between the Danish text and Paraschos' imitation is therefore not relevant.

Marmier in Contemporary Greek cultural life

Let us have a look first on Marmier's position in Greece at the time[27].

As we have seen, Marmier (1808-1892) was the person referred to in the first introduction of Danish literature by K. Pop. Marmier is probably also the one who introduced Andersen in Greece - as elsewhere - by translations of the various articles that he published in the *Revue des deux mondes* and the *Revue de Paris* and in his books on Scandinavian literature. As early as 1837 he wrote an introduction to Andersen's life which together with a translation of Andersen's poem 'The Dead Child' was presented in *Revue de Paris* (October 1838). What interested Marmier was primarily Andersen's life and character, and of his works especially the elegiac poems with their sentimental and religious tone. When Marmier wrote the article, Andersen had published around 10 of his fairytales, they were however neglected by Marmier who as his contemporaries did not comprehend this aspect of Andersen. There is no bibliography or monography of Andersen in Greece, but the impact of Marmier's view on Andersen should definitely be taken into consideration in the Greek tradition[28].

Marmier wrote prose compositions and poems and some of his works

---

[27] On Marmier and Denmark, see P. Høybye, H.C. Andersens franske ven Xavier Marmier, *Studier for Sprog- og Oldtidsforskning* 214, 1950, and more recently K.- E. Høgsbro, A French Visit to a Danish Idyll. Xavier Marmier's Visit to Copenhagen in 1837. In: *The Golden Age revisited. Art and Culture in Denmark 1800-1850,* Copenhagen 1996, 92-99.

[28] Kaplanoglou, op. cit., 191, refers only once to Marmier, discussing the biography presented by Arsinoi Papadopoulou in the review Ἀθηναῖς 1878 'Ο Ανδερσεν διηγούμενος τον βίον εις τον φίλον του Marmier'.

were translated and published in Greek. In one case a translation became the subject of theoretical discussions among contemporary critics on the ethical and didactic value of the French novel in Greek surroundings[29].

I have found no indication that the *Chants populaires du Nord* were translated and published in Greece, although one may say that a translation into Greek around 1863 would have met certain public demands. This means that the text of Marmier must have been communicated somehow, orally or in a Greek written translation, to Paraschos, who needed the assistance of a person who knew French. The identity of this person is a matter of conjecture, but there are many possibilities, the closest his brother Georgios Paraschos, who besides being a poet in his own right was translator of French romantic poetry[30].

The imitations of Paraschos are therefore the result of the following stages of transmission: The texts of Abrahamson-Nyrop-Rahbek (1812) - the translations of Marmier (1842) - a Greek version communicating the texts of Marmier to Paraschos possibly around 1863 - the texts of Paraschos 1863 (publ. 1865) and 1873 (publ. 1876) - the texts of the 1881-edition[31].

---

[29] The work in question was *Ο Φιλάργυρος και ο θησαυρός αυτού. Μυθιστόρημα Ξαυερίου Μαρμιέρου. Μεταφρασθέν υπό Ν. Δεστουνιάνου. Εν Αθήναις, τύποις των Μοϊκανών των Παρισίων*, 1863, cf. Δημ. Γκίνη και Β. Μέξα *Ελληνική Βιβλιογραφία 1800-1860*, τόμος τρίτος, Εν Αθήναις 1957, αρ. 9830 and Σοφία Ντενίση, op. cit., p.91 no. 320. It was discussed in the review *Επτάλοφος* 2, 1863-64, 261, cf. Α. Σαχίνης, *Θεωρία και άγνωστη ιστορία του μυθιστορήματος στην Ελλάδα 1760-1870*, Αθήνα 1992, 77. Among other works by Marmier (the list is not exhaustive) are a French translation of a German short story, turned into Greek by an unknown translator: *Οτιλία, Η εθνική βιβλιοθήκη* Α', 1865, φυλλ. Α'-Ε' (4-8, 12-16, 21-24, 28-32, 37), and *Οι μελλόνυμφοι της Σπιτζεβέργης, Εστία* 2, 1876, 531 ff. (cf. Γιάννης Παπακώστας, *Το περιοδικό Εστία και το διήγημα*, Αθήνα 1982, 158, n. 168).

[30] Cf. Γλ. Πρωτοπαπά-Μπουμπουλίδου, *Γεώργιος Παράσχος, Δωδώνη* (Επιστημ. Επετηρίδα της Φιλοσοφικής Σχολής του Πανεπιστημίου Ιωαννίνων) τομ. έκτος, 1977, 56.

[31] The possibility that Marmier did not know Danish well enough to translate the folk ballads is suggested by Høybye, op. cit., 56, claiming the text of W. Grimm to be the basis for the translation into French. But as a superficial look at the two texts in question shows

Why did Paraschos choose the Danish ballads?

When in 1865 Paraschos published his translation of 'The Dead Knight' in the *Chrysallis* he was still known in Athenian cycles for his youthful opposition to Otho, but was now hastily progressing towards the position as a court poet and the singer of Greek nationalism that he was to enjoy for the rest of his life. His occupation with Danish literature can of course be seen as a step in this direction. And the reason why he chose two Danish folk ballads may of course have been that he found them ready at hand. This may well be so, but it does hardly explain why he considered them worthy to be incorporated in his 1881-edition after a considerable revision.

If we take a closer look at the possible motives for Paraschos to choose the Danish ballads, we shall see that in the contemporary cultural surroundings existed several concomitant factors that may have induced him to this preference. In spite of the often stressed reactionary and classicist features of the Athenian romantics they frequently draw on the Greek folk songs as a source of inspiration and emulation. This implies that choosing the Danish ballads for imitation he might have done so because he saw their close relation to what he knew from indegenous material. And what in Greek tradition comes closest to the two Danish ballads in contents are the popular songs of lament, the *μοιρολόγια*[32]. The circle of motives in this category of Greek folk songs was known to Paraschos and used in several instances - the best moments of his lyrics, according to a prominent Greek critic[33]. In the contemporary collections

---

Marmier had in every case a more comprehensive text to his disposition than that of Grimm, cf. *Altdänische Heldenlieder, Balladen und Märchen*, übersetzt von Wilhelm Carl Grimm, Heidelberg 1811, 73-74 ('Der Ritter Aage und Jungfrau Else'), 147-49 ('Die Mutter im Grabe').

[32] Cf. the description of Marmier of the character of the Danish folk songs: "une poésie âpre et sauvage comme les mœurs qu'elle répresente et les hommes auxquels elle s'adresse...Un rhythme monotone et facile des strophes de deux longs vers qui tombent l'un après l'autre comme deux coups de marteau. Le caractère sombre du Nord la domine du reste complètement, les images riantes y sont rares, les images de deuil y reviennent sans cesse" (Marmier, op. cit, xxxviii).

[33] Ανδρέας Καραντώνης, Από την ποίηση του Αχιλλέα Παράσχου, *Νέα Εστία*, τομ. 110 Χριστ. 1981, 21-38.

of these songs he could find many of the elements of the Danish songs: discussion between the dead mother and her bereaved children[34], two lovers united in the grave, etc[35]. The element of temporary resurrection from death was also known in Greek tradition: in the group of *Songs of Recalling* (Ανακαλέματα) and in the well-known ballad, the 'Song of the Dead Brother'[36]. In his treatment of the Danish ballads Paraschos may well have seen a possibility to show his capability to combine the Danish folk ballads with Greek elements in his own way. For example, he may have found the theme "dead mother called upon by the living to protect the orphan children" in the Greek song where the husband adresses his dead wife:

Σήκω νύφη μου καλή
μη σου γένει προσβολή
σου πάρει άλλη τα κλειδιά
και σου δείρει τα παιδιά

Get up my bride,
lest you be offended
that another may take the keys [that is take your place in the house] and beat up your children[37].

In the Greek tradition the mother renounces - she is no more able to stand up, but in the Danish ballad she does. Paraschos found here a motive that could be elaborated and combined with his own way of writing poetry.

And finally, the theme and motives were inherent to the poetry of Greek romanticism which has been characterised as a churchyard poetry concerned with the subjects nekrophaneia and necrophilia as some of

---

[34] *Τραγούδια ρωμαίικα. Popularia carmina Graeciae recentioris* edidit Arnoldus Passow, Lipsiae 1860, no. 260 ('Η μήτηρ αποθαμμένη').
[35] Σπ. Ζαμπέλιος, *Άσματα δημοτικά της Ελλάδος*, Κέρκυρα 1852, 155, Passow, op. cit., no. 415.
[36] Cf. G. Saunier, *Ελληνικά δημοτικά τραγούδια. Τα μοιρολόγια*, Αθήνα 1999, 192-95 and the correspondent texts. On the 'Song of the Dead Brother', see *Το δημοτικό τραγούδι. Παραλογές*, επιμ. Γιώργος Ιωάννου, Αθήνα 1975, 31-43.
[37] The example is taken from G. Saunier, op. cit., 84.

its most popular issues.

It is therefore evident that Paraschos would find the Danish folk ballads congenial to his own poetry and to that of the Greek *moirologia*. What must have crossed his mind is the fact that the Danish folk ballad has an epic dimension comparable to that of the Greek ballads proper (the παραλογές, to which the 'Song of the Dead Brother' belongs), and this element may well be what he saw as a challenge. The result is not bad and the popularity of the imitation and the subject may be seen from the fact that 'A Mother's Return' was published also in the review of the coming generation *Estia*, which indicates that the theme of the Danish ballad in its Paraschian form was acceptable to Nikolaos Politis and the folklore movement[38].

A comparison of the texts of Marmier and Paraschos.

A complete analysis of the imitations of Paraschos will fall outside the scope of this study, but with the comparative texts in the Appendices as a basis some conclusions may be ventured on a general as well as on a more specific level[39].

Generally, when Paraschos translates the text of Marmier he gives a fairly close and adequate translation.

In ignorance of the original Danish text and faced with the prose character of his model, Paraschos chose the iambic fifteen-syllable "political verse", the metre of the Greek folk song, with no stanzaic structure, but united in rhymed couplets.

In long passages, more so in 'The Dead Knight' than in 'A Mother's Return', he gives his own additions, which are usually either descriptions - a feature seldom met in the Danish ballad tradition - or an extension of the dialogue to reach a more dramatic effect by way of suspense. In his additions he took inspiration from Greek folk poetry.

Innovations are additions of adjectives, e.g. in 'A Mother's Return' l.

---

[38] *Εστία* Α', 1876, 191-92.
[39] It is evident that my remarks on how Paraschos treated the Danish folk ballads should be substantiated by analysis of the remaining part of his translations as well as of the practise of imitation by the Athenian romantics.

64 τρομασμένα and άγριο σκοτάδι, and introductory clauses, as in l. 43 of the same ballad "της είπε πικραμένα".

Many additions are caused by rhyme, cf. 'A Mother's Return' l., 10, 11, 21, 37, which means that the innovations of Paraschos are often to be found in the second hemistic, e.g. in the same ballad l. 39 ακουμπισμένη, l. 43 πικραμένα and l. 44 σαν κ' εμένα.

The desire for more effectful and dramatic expressions, which is characteristic of his own original poetry, led him to divide the songs in "scenes" or "acts". These "Paraschian" parts share virtues and faults with his own personal lyric as well as that of his contemporaries.

Comparing the two imitations, there seems to be a notable difference in quality: More than in 'The Dead Knight', Paraschos managed in 'A Mother's Return' to give an even and smooth rendering of his model, whereas his own inspiration in several places found lucky and ingenouos expressions in his additions and interpretations.

The language in both songs may be characterised as light καθαρεύουσα, on the same stylistic level both in the dialogue and in the narrative parts.

The desire for reaching a more powerful and dramatic way of expression is a general feature. However, in some cases, Paraschos seems to have felt that he was overdoing it, changed his mind and reached a more subdued expression, closer to his model. This is seen most remarkedly in the final parts of both imitations, cf. below.

The changes made by Paraschos in the definitive versions of the edition of 1881 gave a better text, presenting in several instances a language more smooth and vernacular with more successful poetic expressions - and closer to the Danish original he had not seen. One may venture the conclusion that Paraschos in the intervening period had come to a closer relationship to the spirit of the Danish folk song. An instance of this is that he in the final 1881-version decided to include what he had left out in the earlier version: The beautiful and expressive scene in 'The Dead Knight' where Else combs the knight's hair (l. 23-26).

Remarks on 'The Dead Knight'

In l. 5 Paraschos extends the description of the grief of Else, giving it a more Greek and tragic flavour:

Η Έλση κλαίει και σκληρώς
την κεφαλήν της κρούει,
Else weeps and beats her head.

In l. 7-8 Paraschos adds two lines on his own account to enhance the effect of the resurrection. They are Paraschian poetry at its worst:

Τα εσπαρμένα του οστά
μετά σπουδής συνάζει,
Τα συναρμόζει τρίζοντα,
τους σκώληκας τινάζει,
He gathers eagerly his scattered bones
he assembles them creakingly
shaking off the worms.

Another example of this is l. 30, where Κροτούντων των οδόντων του απο θανάτου ψύχος "with teeth crunching from the cold of death" is a Paraschian innovation.

In l. 12 the apparently contradicting expression την παρθένον χήραν (maiden widow), is an example of the apparent oxymoron, a rhetoric device much loved by Paraschos in his art poetry. Marmier has "jeune fille".

In l. 21-22 we have the remarkable statement of Else:
Είν' αληθές, είσαι νεκρός,
σε ήλλαξε το χώμα,
Πλην τώρα, τώρα, σ' αγαπώ
πλειότερον ακόμα.
It is really true, you are dead!
the earth has changed you,
but now, now,
I love you even more.

This is written by the poet Paraschos who wanted his loved one to be 'by sickness slain', to dig up his dear dead father to see what time had done to him, in short what made among others Andreas Karantonis characterize him as the most *unrestrained* (ακράτητος) of the Athenian romantics[40]. But it is significant to note that this is an example of several to show how Paraschos simply overdid the rich imagery of the Greek folk song:

Αν έχης χνώτα, θέλω σε, και μυρωδιά, 'γαπώ σε,
Κι αν ήσαι κι απ' την μαύρη γη, μυριοπαρακαλώ σε.
If you have the breath and smell [of death] I love you,
And if you come from the black earth,
I beg you a thousand times [to stand up and join us][41].

Another example of the desire towards more effectful expressions is l. 25-26, when - after the combing scene which obviously appealed to the Greek poet - he presents the heroine in a more intense and psychologically more complex situation than did the text of Marmier:

Δακρύων χύνει χείμαρρον, και μειδιά και κλαίει,
Και της βραδείας του πνοής το ψύχος αναπνέει.
She cries a torrent of tears
and smiling and crying
she inhales the coldness of his slow breath.

The paradox in the apparently antithetical smiling-through-tears figure was very popular with Paraschos:

υπόδακρυς την έβλεπε και τη προσεμειδία
η Παναγία δι' αυτόν ελέγετο Μαρία.
He smiled through tears at her,
to him the Virgin was called Maria[42].

In the following long passage of pure Paraschian vintage we get a dra-

---

[40] Ανδρέας Καραντώνης, op. cit., 35. The poems to which I refer, are ''Έρως' (cited from Ποιηταί του ΙΘ' αιώνος, Βασ. Βιβλ. 12, 1955, 276) and 'Πόθος' (1863), Ποιήματα Β', 1881, 357-58. The wish to exhume or be exhumed is found in several songs, see Ελληνικά δημοτικά τραγούδια, Βασ. Βιβλ. 47, 1959, 237, no. 44 A and B (from the collections of Lelekos and Laskaris).
[41] Passow, op. cit., no. 357.
[42] Ο άγνωστος ποιητής, Ποιήματα Α', 1881, 11.

matic dialogue and in the knight's description of the life in the tomb (l. 34), Paraschos adds a Christian dimension to his imitation, alien to the Greek tradition of folk poetry and the Danish ballad:

> Εκεί, ρεμβάζομεν
> και τον Θεόν ζητούμεν.
> There we live in reverie, seeking God[43].

The same motive is pursued in the next passage l. 37-38, where the knight is asked:

> Αλλοίμονον· είναι βαρύ επάνω σας το μνήμα;
> Woe, does your tomb weigh heavily on you?

and answers:

> Πολύ βαρύ· όμως πολύ βαρύτερον το κρίμα
> It is very heavy
> but even more heavy is the sin.

This dialogue is well-known in Greek folk songs. In the song published by Fauriel 'The Cry from the Tomb' ('Η βοή του μνήματος'), the dead is addressed and answers as follows:

> - Μήνα το χώμα σου βαρεί; μήνα η μαύρη πλάκα;
> - Ουδέ το χώμα μου βαρεί, ουδέ η μαύρη πλάκα,
> μόν' το 'χω μάραν κ' εντροπήν, κ' έναν καϋμόν μεγάλον,
> το πώς με καταφρόνεσες
> Does the earth lie heavily on you, does the tombstone,
> Neither does the earth, nor the tombstone,
> but I feel worried and ashamed, and deeply sorrow,
> because you affronted me...[44]

In the Paraschian version the knight is referring not to an insult hurt-

---

[43] "ρεμβάζομεν" was originally πλανώμεθα in the *Chrysallis*-version. The words are closely connected in the poetic vocabulary of Paraschos, cf. Ο άγνωστος ποιητής, *Ποιήματα*, Α', 1881, 14: Δεν έζη· ωνειρεύετο, ρεμβάζων επλανάτο, and Επιορκία, *Ποιήματα*, Α', 1881, 189: Εις το πεδίον τ' όμμα του ρεμβώδες επλανάθη.
[44] Claude Fauriel, *Chants populaires de la Grèce moderne*, Paris 1824 (= C.F., Δημοτικά τραγούδια της συγχρόνου Ελλάδος, Αθήνα 1956, 327).

ing his pride, but to sin, that is a religious Christian element not to be found in the Danish folk ballad, where their is no sin and consequently no redemption.

Line 40 was changed by Paraschos from the somewhat lame text of the Chrysallis version

> Τί κάμνεις, τί, εις το ψυχρόν και ζοφερόν σου στρώμα;
> How are you doing on your cold and gloomy coach?

into the psychologically more probable question:

> Τί κάμνεις;... μ' αναπολείς κ' υπό την γην ακόμα;
> How are you? Do you think of me, even below the earth?

which is naturally what interests Else most: Does he, that is: is he able to love her still and is his love so strong that he can love her even from the grave, outre tombe? The question serves as an introduction to a longer Paraschian passage where the two lovers exchange information about their abodes respectively. While the interrogation carries reminiscenses of Greek traditional lament, this section of the poem contains lines of poetic beauty and pure inspiration. It marks the end and dramatic climax of the scene in the house of Else, when she falls in his arms as an answer to his question if she does still love him (l. 51-52):

> Η κόρη εις την αγκάλην του
> την κρύαν εβυθίσθη,
> Και η ζωή τον θάνατον
> Θερμώς ενηγκαλίσθη.
>
> the maid sank into his frozen arms,
> and life did warmly death embrace..

Note that the text was changed from the version of the Chrysallis, which ran:

> εις τους κόλπους του θρηνούσα εβυθίσθη.
> she sank into his arms with grief.

The definitive version manages to convey the effective antithesis between the cold embrace of death and the warm of life.

In the first version of the ballad the graveyard entourage was further elaborated in the final act, where the text in Paraschos' first version goes (l. 67-71):

> Και όταν, όταν έφθασαν το μέλαν δάσος, ότε
> εφάνησαν τα μνήματα, υπερφυείς ιππόται,
> κεκαλυμμένοι σάβανα λευκότερα χιόνος,
> ίππευον ίππων σκελετούς κ' εκάλπαζαν αφώνως.
> το δάσος έγεμε σκιών και το νεκροταφείον,
> And when, when they reached the dark forest, when
> the tombs appeared, gigantic knights
> covered by shrouds more white than snow
> rode skeleton horses in silent pace.

In the definitive version Paraschos removed the spectacular ride of the giant knights on the skeleton horses - for which one may suspect a specific model - and chose a text nearer to the French text:

> Και σιωπώντας έφθασαν
> εις το νεκροταφείον,
> του Αζ η κόμη έπεσεν
> εξαίφνης η πλουσία·
> Και ότε πάλιν η μικρά
> εφάνη εκκλησία,
> Η όψις του ωχρίασε,
> Και τεθλιμμένος εις σταυρόν
> μνημείου επλησίασε!
> And in silence they reached the churchyard,
> and suddenly fell the rich hair of Aage,
> and when the small church again did appear,
> his face went grey
> and broken down he went to a cross of a tomb[45].

Finally, in l. 78 the addition of Paraschos

---

[45] For emphasis Paraschos here breaks the metrical construction, l. 71-72 consisting of three first hemistichs. For the same emphasis in a parallel situation, cf. *Επιορκία*, 200: "Νύκτα κ' ημέραν, πάντοτε, την έβλεπες πλησίον/εις το κενόν μνημείον, /Κ' εις τον σταυρόν του μνήματος ερείδετο, ωραία/ Ως δάσους φθινοπωρινού η τεθλιμμένη θέα".

Εθρήνει μόνον ο βορράς
εις τας ιτέας πνέων!

And only the northern wind was lamenting in the willows
closes dramatically the scene. The French text only concludes: "she did not see him any more", perhaps with greater effect[46].

Remarks on 'A Mother's Return'

The Danish original had two lyrical refrains in each stanza. They were not translated by Marmier whose purpose was apparently only to present the narrative parts of the ballad.

Dyring and his wife have been replaced by the Konstantinos / Konstantis and the slender maid of the Greek folk ballad.

Note that the formular expression of the Danish folk ballad "under Ø", tranlated by Marmier in both cases, is rendered by Paraschos only here. It literally means "under an island", not "dans une île", or "σ' ένα νησί", but has in Danish (Scandinavian) language of folk songs simply the meaning "to go far away", which Marmier may or may not have known - Paraschos and his communicator certainly did not, as is shown by the repetition of the formular in l. 7:

Άλλη γυναίκ' απ' το νησί
ο Κωνσταντίνος παίρνει·

Constantine took another wife from the island.

In l. 3 the comparison of the lovers to the flowers is unfamiliar to the language of the folk ballad, but not the allegoric identification. It has a formular character, however, and can be testified other places in the Paraschian corpus, where the lily represents chastity and fertility, e.g. in the epic poem Alfredos we find a variant of the formular:

Κ' ενθουσιών διήρχετο πλησίον της τον βίον
Ως χρυσαλίς εις κάλυκα. ως μύρον εις το κρίνον.

And he spend his life happily at her side,
like a butterfly in a cocoon, like myrrh in the lily[47].

---

[46] For the northwind expressing grief in the poetry of Paraschos, see Ο άγνωστος ποιητής, Άπαντα Α', 1881, 20: "Πολλάκις ότε ο βορράς εθρήνει".
[47] Άπαντα Α', 1881, 59.

In l. 5-6 the death of the wife is described by Paraschos as follows:

Μα γείνηκε κατάμαυρο ο Χάρος χελιδόνι,
Και μιαν αυγή τη λυγερή πηγαίνει και λαβόνει.
But death became a swallow black as night
and one morning he goes and takes the maid,

This metaphor is easily testified in the folk songs, e.g.:

Κι ο Χάρος έγινε πουλί σα μαύρο χελιδόνι,
επέταξε και στην καρδιά σαΐτεψε την κόρη.
And Death became a bird, as a black swallow
and threw in flight an arrow in the heart of the maid[48].

In the following scene, maybe the most beautiful and moving in the two imitations, Paraschos balances between the responsibility towards the model and his own inspiration, as in l. 24:

Γιατί μια μάνα και νεκρή
μπορεί ν' ακούση ακόμα.
Because a mother, even dead,
is able still to hear..

Which reminds a Dane of the mother in Andersen's the 'History of a Mother', who when asked by Death how she managed to reach the greenhouse first, simply states: "I am a mother".

In the same way exalting the power of motherly love that casts light even in the realm of the dead is the brilliant l. 28:

Και το Θεό με της στοργής
το φως πηγαίνει να βρη...
And with the light of motherly care
she goes to find God.

Equally strong is the metaphor of the dead mother sleeping with Death who has taken over the place of her husband, their father (l. 48):

Οπού ο Χάρος κοίτεται
μερόνυχτα μαζή μου.

---

[48] cf. Passow, op. cit., nos. 296, 417 (= Fauriel, op. cit. II 112), Saunier, op. cit., 408.

where Death does sleep with me
by day and night.

That the dead woman is married to Death is also part of the figurative language of the Greek folk song:

Εψές εγώ παντρεύθηκα, εψές αργά το βράδυ.
Ο άδης είν' ο άντρας μου, η πλάκ' η πεθερά μου.
Last night I married, late last night,
Hades is my husband, the tombstone my mother-in-law[49].

Further additions, which in this imitation seem appropriate and psychologically in line with the characters, are l. 26, where the children go to her coffin φέρετρο), thus effectively confronting the mother with their grief, and l. 36 where she is described as trying to remember the way to her house.

In the ultimate confrontation between the mother and the negligent father, the first part of her monologue is rendered faithfully, but the final threat and the description of the mother defending her children (l. 65-66) are much more dramatic and expressive in the Paraschian version and suggest the encounter of Don Giovanni with the stoneguest in Mozart's opera[50].

Έχε το νου σου, Κωνσταντή!..
και της νεκρής το μάτι
Φωσφόρισε στα σκοτεινά
Beware, o Konstantis!
and the eyes of the dead
were shining luminously in the dark.

As in 'The Dead Knight', Paraschos changed in the final part of the 'Mother's Return' (l. 67-69) his original concept and ended up with a solution closer to the original. From the version in the *Byron*

Εκεί τ' ορνίθι άρχησε στα σκοτεινά να κράζη

---

[49] Passow, op. cit., no. 374.
[50] Paraschos seems in several instances, especially in his epics (e.g. the *Alfredos*), to have been inspired by scenic representations.

και θάρρευες πως τη νεκρή από μακριά φωνάζει.
Τ' άκουσε κι ανατρίχιασε, εστράφηκε, εστάθη,
The cock began to crow in the darkness,
so you would say he was calling the dead from afar,
she heard it, shivered, turned around, and stopped

to the 1881-edition:

Οι θύρες, είπε, τ' ουρανού ανοίξανε, χαράζει·
Το μαύρο ορνίθι ελάλησε και τ' άσπρο με φωνάζει,
Να μείνω περισσότερο δεν ημπορώ.
The doors of heaven open, it is dawn, she said,
the black cock crowed, the white is calling me,
I cannot further stay.

Did the Danish ballads in any way influence the poetry of Paraschos?

I do not think that it is possible to demonstrate with safety that Paraschos in specific poems took inspiration from the Danish ballads. So far Timoleon Philemon is probably right[51]. But I find it evident that he in his poetry, which in those years came to include the epic poems, had the Danish ballads in the form to which he had converted them as a constant source of inspiration together with other related poetry.

The theme of the two ballads is expressed several times in Paraschian poetry, e.g. explicitly when he presents his heroine Lydia in the epic poem of the same name, composed in 1863 at the time he was working on the Danish ballads, saying:

Α, η αγάπη καταργεί το κράτος του θανάτου
Oh, love does conquer the realm of Death[52].

This is a conclusion that can of course be drawn from the Danish ballads, but is hardly more than a general reflection. In the same way the motive of the two lovers united in the grave is developed in the same poem, when Lydia visions her union and marriage with her lover in the grave:

---

[51] See n. 15 above.
[52] Άπαντα Α', 1881, 156.

Ω μήτερ μου· όταν κλεισθή το διαυγές του όμμα,
Θα αφήσω τα μεσάνυκτα του τάφου μου το χώμα,
Και θα υπάγω εις αυτού τον τάφον να τελέσω
Τον σιγαλόν υμέναιον και παρ' αυτώ να πέσω.
Oh, mother, when his bright eyes are closed,
by midnight shall I leave my grave,
to go to him to celebrate
in silence the sacred vows of marriage,
and go to rest united with him in one grave[53].

However, the poem which in contents and expressions comes closest to the Danish ballads in the Paraschian versions is the epic *Perjury* (*Επιορκία*) from 1873. A short summary of the plot will make this clear:

We are given safe indications as to the time and place of the action: The heroine and hero (Ida and Vrasidas) live in a tower (πύργος) in the mountains outside Athens at the time of the great Cretan revolts in the 1860'es. In spite of that, the setting of the poem is a semimythical landscape and the central characters are more like the prince and princess of the fairytale.

They are separated by the revolt in Crete, in which Vrasidas feels he must take part. The separation is described as taking place just a month after their engagement:

Ακόμα είναι σύζυγοι μιας σελήνης μόνον
they had been married only one month[54],

which may (or may not) be a reflection of 'The Dead Knight', where the separation takes place also after a month (l. 3)[55]. Although Vrasidas tries to avert it, Ida insists before they part to swear that she will continue to love him even if he dies:

---

[53] Ibid.157. Cf. the motive Ο γάμος εις τον Άδη, Passow, op. cit., no. 370.
[54] Ibid., 163.
[55] Note that Else's death is also supposed to happen within a month (l. 80), and that Ida begins to feel anxious about the fate of Brasidas after a month: Παρήλθε μην αφ' ης ο νέος... Παρήλθε μην· εις μην και μόνον (p. 171).

> Ορκίζομαι εις τον Θεόν τον αληθή και ζώντα,
> Αείποτε να σ' αγαπώ, ακόμη και θανόντα
> I swear by the true and living God
> that I shall love you always, even if you die[56].

The oath returns returns several times during the poem as a *Leitmotif*, and when he finally dies, it is rephrased. As in 'The Dead Knight' (l. 22) her love is now even greater after his death:

> Αείποτε να σ' αγαπώ, πλειότερον θανόντα
> I shall love you always, even more now you have died[57].

Vrasidas has taken his own life on the plain of Vafes in Crete, when he understands that the battle is lost. She laments him in a cenotaph, but despite her grief she falls in love with another young man, and although she fights against it she finally surrenders and is so guilty of perjury. The night of their wedding coincides with the All Souls' Day, Ψυχοσάββατο (in the orthodox tradition the Saturday before the first Sunday of the Lent), by Paraschos called "The Easter of the Dead" ("Το Πάσχα των θανόντων"). The dead Vrasidas, uncared for in opposition to his fellow victims of the battle, goes to the house of wedding. He kills her new lover by his mere breath, takes his shape and goes to confront Ida. The scene where she gradually realises that this is not her new husband but the dead lover reminds in various ways of the scene in 'The Dead Knight': the dead seeks to warm himself by the fire, the abode in the grave is described as narrow, and the dialogue between the dead and living person may owe something to the parallel dialogue in 'The Dead Knight'. The same may be said of the next phase where the dead knight takes Ida from the burning tower and is united with her in a cold embrace:

> Αλλ' ακουσίως τας ψυχράς αγκάλας του ανοίγει
> και την εναγκαλίζεται.
> But unwillingly he opens his cold bosom
> and embraces her[58].

---

[56] Ibid., 169.
[57] Ibid., 200.
[58] Ibid., 253.

After that, he takes her to Crete, and the ride to his grave is most probably a reflection of the ride of Leonora to the grave of William in Bürger's *Lenore*. This famous international lament of art poetry, itself influenced by and influencing songs of folk tradition, will have been known to Paraschos in accessible Greek translations. To our purpose it is relevant to note that Bürger's ballad in 1863 was translated with a thorough introduction in the *Chrysallis* by one of Paraschos' colleagues, Angelos Vlachos[59].

While love does certainly play a part in *Perjury*, the return of the lover happens not as a result of the loss of love as in 'The Dead Knight', but because she fails to keep her oath.

When Paraschos set out to write his epic, he intended to combine a patriotic poem with a lovestory[60]. He did not have a single model in his mind, but as in the describing of the national fight for freedom he draws on the heavily nationalistic poetry of his age, he took inspiration from what he found in popular literature to describe the lovestory. This included local popular tradition as he found it in the songs of lament and the ballads of the Greek people, as well as foreign poetry. Besides Bürger's *Lenore*, 'The Dead Knight' and 'A Mother's Return' in the French translation belonged to this last category.

---

[59] *Χρυσαλλίς* Α' (1863) 271-77. Vlachos' purpose was mainly to show the differences between the poem of Bürger and the Greek 'Song of the Dead Brother'. On Bürger in Greece, see Κίρκη Κεφαλέα, Οι ελληνικές εκδοχές της 'Λεονώρας' του Μπύργκερ, *Πόρφυρας* 89, 1999, 362-74, and Γιάννης Δάλλας, Μια ακόμα μετάφραση της 'Λεονώρας', *Πόρφυρας* 91, 1999, 63-70. On Bürger in Denmark and Scandinavia, see Aage Kabell, DgF 90 and the Danish Novel, *Scandinavica* VI, 1967, 86-94.

[60] The poem is by common consent considered the best of the epics, cf. the estimation of Palamas, *Άπαντα* IB', 269-74).

Appendix I
Synoptic comparison of
Marmier, Aage et Else ~ Paraschos, Ο ΝΕΚΡΟΣ ΙΠΠΟΤΗΣ[61]:

X. Marmier, *Chants populaires du Nord*, Paris 1842, 108-111:	Α. Παράσχος, *Ποιήματα*, Α΄, Αθήνα 1881, 311-314:
Aage et Else	Ο ΝΕΚΡΟΣ ΙΠΠΟΤΗΣ (Κατά το Δανικόν) Μίμησις
	Α΄
Le chevalier Aage s'en va dans une île,	1 Την νύκτα ο ιππότης Αζ τον ίππον του λαμβάνει,
et se fiance avec Else, la belle jeune fille.	2 Κ' εις την πατρίδα την αυγήν της νέας Έλσης φθάνει.
Il se fiance richement avec Else, la belle. Un mois après,	3 Τους αρραβώνας του τελεί, πλην μην παρήλθε μόνον
il était enseveli dans la tombe noir.	4 Κ' υπό την μαύρην γην ο Αζ κοιμάται των δρυμώνων.
Else se regrette amèrement.	5 Η Έλση κλαίει και σκληρώς την κεφαλή της κρούει,
Sous sa couche de terre le chevalier l'entend qui soupire.	6 Ο Αζ, από την κλίνην του την κάτω την ακούει,
	7 Τα εσπαρμένα του οστά μετά σπουδής συνάζει,
	8 Τα συναρμόζει τρίζοντα, τους σκώληκας τινάζει,
Il se lève. Il prend son cercueil sur ses épaules	9 Κ' εγείρεται, το φέρετρον λαμβάνων εις το ώμον,
et se dirige vers sa demeure.	10 Και βαίνει προς της παλαιάς αγάπης του τον δρόμον...

---

[61] I have for practical reasons divided the text of Paraschos in two hemistichs. The numbering is mine. The text is that of the 1881-edition, which in some places is different from that of the periodicals. These differences are noted as an appendix to the appendix.

Il frappe à la porte
avec son cercueil:
- Lève-toi, jeune fille, dit-il.
Ouvre ta chambre à ton fiancé. -
- Non, répond Else, je n'ouvrirai pas,
 	
à moins que tu ne puisses, comme autrefois,
prononcer le nom de Jésus.
- Lève-toi, dit-il, et ouvre la porte.
Je puis, comme autrefois, prononcer .
le nom de Jésus
	11 Κτυπά με το φορείον του
	   του οίκου της την θύραν
	12 -Ανοιξον, Έλση! έκραξε
	   προς την παρθένον χήραν.
	13 -Αν είσαι συ ο ίδιος,
	   εκείνος εάν είσαι,
	14 Ω! Του Χριστού το όνομα
	   να είπης μη αρνήσαι!
	15 -Άνοιξε, κόρη! Του Χριστού
	   το όνομα προφέρω,
	
	16 Μ' εκούρασεν ο οίκος μου,
	   ον εις τους ώμους φέρω.

	———

Else se lève avec des larmes sur les joues.
Else ouvre la porte
au mort,
et le fait entrer.
	17 Ο έρως υπερίσχυσεν·
	   ανοίγει παραφόρως
	18 Την θύραν, και ο ζοφερός
	   εισήλθεν οδοιπόρος.
	19 Πλήρης χαράς εις την λευκήν
	   τον έθλιψεν αγκάλην.
	20 -Ω, Αζ! συ είσαι συ!
	   μοι απεδόθης πάλιν!
	21 Είν' αληθές, είσαι νεκρός,
	   σε ήλλαξε το χώμα,
	22 Πλην τώρα, τώρα, σ' αγαπώ
	   πλειότερον ακόμα!

	———

Elle prend un peigne d'or et le passe dans
la chevelure de son bien-aimé.
A chaque cheveu qu'elle
enlève,
elle verse d'abondantes larmes.
	23 Με τους λευκούς δακτύλους της
	   την κόμην του κτενίζει,
	24 Κ' εις πάσαν τρίχα του χρυσήν
	   ην τρέμουσα χωρίζει,
	25 Δακρύων χύνει χείμαρρον,
	   και μειδιά και κλαίει,
	26 Και της βραδείας του πνοής
	   το ψύχος αναπνέει.
	
	Β΄
	27 Σιωπηλός την έβλεπεν...
	   αφήκε το φορείον,

- Mon bien-aimé, mon cher Aage, dit-elle,
raconte-moi comment tu te trouves
dans la terre sombre.

Chaque fois, répond Aage, que tu es d'une
humeur joyeuse, ma tombe est entourée
de feuilles
de roses. Chaque fois que tu pleures,
je vois tomber
dans mon cercueil des gouttes de sang.

28 Κ' εις την εστίαν ώρμησε
   να θερμανθή πλησίον...
29 Ενηγκαλίσθη την πυράν,
   κ' ηκούετο ο ήχος,
30 Κροτούντων των οδόντων του
   από θανάτου ψύχος.
31 -Έλση! - Ω! λάλει· άνοιξε
   τα κεκλεισμένα χείλη,
32 Και πάλιν εις την Έλσην σου,
   ως άλλοτε ομίλει!
33 -Απέμαθον να ομιλώ!
   ημείς, δεν ομιλούμεν...
34 -Ω Αζ!.. - Εκεί, ρεμβάζομεν
   και τον θεόν ζητούμεν.
35 -Κ' εγώ να έλθω, λάβε με
   μαζή σου· ευσπλαγχνία!
36 -Είναι στενά, πολύ στενά
   και ψύχος και σκοτία.
37 -Αλλοίμονον· είναι βαρύ
   επάνω σας το μνήμα;
38 -Πολύ βαρύ· όμως πολύ
   βαρύτερον το κρίμα...
39 -Ειπέ με, Αζ, αγάπη μου,
   υπό το μαύρον χώμα,
40 Τί κάμνεις;... με αναπολείς
   κ' υπό την γην ακόμα;
41 -Οταν δεν κλαίης, μου κοσμούν

   το φέρετρον μυρσίναι,

42 Αλλ' όμως πλήρες αίματος,
   οπόταν κλαίης είναι...
43 -Ω! σιγά! -Όμως, λέγε με,
   ο ήλιός σας, κόρη,
44 Ακόμη λάμπει, χύνει φως
   και θάλπος εις τα όρη;
45 -Ναι λάμπει! - Ημείς, ήλιον
   δεν έχομεν... Ακόμα
46 Θερμαίνει και ζωογονεί
   και παγωμένον σώμα;
47 -Θερμαίνει μόνον ευτυχείς!
   -Ημάς δεν μας θερμαίνει!

	48 Κ' έχετε ρόδα πάντοτε, ω Έλση πεφιλμένη; 49 Την έβλεπε, την έβλεπε με το βαθύ του όμμα· 50 Εξαίφνης· - Έλση, έκραξε, με αγαπάς ακόμα; 51 Η κόρη εις την αγκάλην του την κρύαν εβυθίσθη, 52 Και η ζωή τον θάνατον θερμώς ενηγκαλίσθη... 53 Αίφνης φωνή αντήχησεν εν μέσω των ανέμων· 54 Ηγέρθη, την απώθησε και ηκροάτο τρέμων...
- Voila que le coq rouge chante. Il faut que je te quitte. Tous les morts retournent en terre. Je dois m'en aller avec eux.	55 - Με κράζει, είπεν, ο λευκός αλέκτωρ από κάτω 56 Με λέγει, ότι την ζωήν ην έκλεψα ταράττω... 57 Πηγαίνω, μη τον άρχοντα του σκότους παροργίσω, 58 Ω, πόσον είσθε ευτυχείς οι μένοντες οπίσω... 59 Η Έλση τον εμπόδισε μ' απελπισίας σχήμα. 60 -Μη κλαίης, μη! είναι βαρύ, είναι μεγάλον κρίμα! 61 Αφες να φύγω, με καλούν, εσήμανεν η ώρα· 62 Ακούεις;.. και ο ερυθρός
Voilà que le coq noir chante. Il faut que je descende dans mon tombeau. Les portes du ciel sont ouvertes. Il faut que je te dise adieu. Le chevalier se lève, prend son cercueil sur son dos, et s'avance avec peine du coté du cimetière; car Else est désolée, et s'en va avec celui qu'elle aime à travers la forêt obscure. Et quand ils eurent traversé la forêt	αλέκτωρ κράζει τώρα. 63 Επί των ώμων κατηφής λαμβάνει το φορείον, 64 Και προχωρεί κλονούμενος εις το νεκροταφείον. 65 Ήτον απαρηγόρητος, διότι η μνηστή του, 66 Απεγνωσμένη, κλαίουσα, εβάδιζε μαζί του... 67 Αλλ' ότε, ότε άφησαν το δάσος το πλησίον

et qu'ils arrivèrent dans la cimetière les cheveux dorés d'Aage pâlirent. Et quand ils eurent traversé le cimétière et qu'ils entrèrent dans l'église, les joues roses d'Aage pâlirent.	68 Και σιωπώντας έφθασαν εις το νεκροταφείον, 69 Του Αζ η κόμη έπεσεν εξαίφνης η πλουσία· 70 Και ότε πάλιν η μικρά
Écoute, dit-il, écoute Else, ma bien-aimée. Ne pleure plus sur ton fiancé. Lève les yeux au ciel, et vois comme il est beau avec toutes ses étoiles. Elle lève les yeux au ciel. Elle regarde les étoiles. Pendant ce temps, le mort descend dans son caveau.	εφάνη εκκλησία, 71 Η όψις του ωχρίασε, 72 Και τεθλιμμένος εις σταυρόν μνημείου επλησίασε! 73 -Άκουσον, Έλση! μη θρηνής, αγάπη μου ματαίως· 74 Ιδέ, ιδέ τον ουρανόν οπόσον είν' ωραίος! 75 Κ' εν ω η κόρη ένδακρυς, ανύψωνε το βλέμμα, 76 Εκείνος εις το μνήμα του εισέδυσεν ηρέμα... 77 Ότε το κατεβίβασε τον Αζ δεν είδε πλέον, 78 Εθρήνει μόνον ο βορράς εις τας ιτέας πνέων!
Elle ne le revit plus.	
La jeune fille retourne tristement dans sa demeure. Un mois après, elle était ensevelie dans la terre sombre.	79 Κ' εστράφη με κλονούμενον εις την οικίαν βήμα· 80 Παρήλθε μην, και ήνοιξαν και δι' εκείνην μνήμα. 1863

Paraschos 1865 and 1881

A collation of the two editions: *Χρυσαλλίς* Γ΄ 1865, 653-54 (Χ) and *Ποιήματα* 1881, 311-14 (Π) shows the following differences. Orthographic differences have not been registered. The text in X, which is not divided into sections, carried the dedication: Αφιερούται τη Μαρία.

l. 1: ῍Αζ (Χ) > ᾽Αζ (Π).
l. 15: άνοιξον (Χ) > άνοιξε (Π)
l. 19: έθλιβεν (Χ) > έθλιψεν (Π)
l. 20: είσαι ο ίδιος! (Χ) > συ είσαι, είσαι συ (Π)
l. 23-26: The scene with the combing is missing in X.
l. 27: Δεν ήνοιξε τα χείλη του (Χ) > Σιωπηλός την έβλεπεν.. (Π)
l. 31: άνοιξον (Χ) > άνοιξε (Π)
l. 32: Και πάντοτε ομίλει μου, και πάντοτε ομίλει! (Χ) > Και πάλιν εις την Ελσην σου, ως άλλοτε ομίλει! (Π).
l. 33: εκεί δεν ομιλούμεν (Χ) > ημείς, δεν ομιλούμεν. (Π)
l. 34: Μόνον πλανώμεθα και (Χ) > Εκεί, ρεμβάζομεν και (Π)
l. 35: -Λάβε με, λάβε με με σε! ω, Αζ μου, ευσπλαγχνία (Χ) > Κ᾽ εγώ να έλθω, λάβε με μαζή σου· ευσπλαγχνία! (Π)
l. 37: το χώμα εις το μνήμα (Χ) > επάνω σας το μνήμα (Π)
l. 40: Τί κάμνεις, τί, εις το ψυχρόν και ζοφερόν σου στρώμα; (Χ) > Τί κάμνεις;.. μ᾽ αναπολείς κ᾽ υπό την γην ακόμα; (Π)
l. 43: Έλση, λέγε με (Χ) > Όμως, λέγε με (Π)
l. 44: Εξέρχεται ως άλλοτε και λάμπει εις τα όρη; (Χ) > Ακόμη λάμπει, χύνει φως και θάλπος εις τα όρη; (Π)
l. 46: παν (Χ) > και (Π)
l. 51: εις τους κόλπους του θρηνούσα εβυθίσθη (Χ) > εις την αγκάλην του την κρύαν εβυθίσθη (Π)
l. 53: Τότε (Χ) > Αίφνης (Π)
l. 61: αντήχησεν (Χ) > εσήμανεν (Π)
l. 62: ερυθρούς (Χ) > ερυθρός (Π)
l. 63: έλαβε και πάλε το φορείον (Χ) > κατηφής λαμβάνει το φορείον (Π)
l. 64: προς (Χ) > εις (Π)
l. 67-71:
Και όταν, όταν έφθασαν το μέλαν δάσος, ότε
εφάνησαν τα μνήματα, υπερφυείς ιππόται,
κεκαλυμμένοι σάβανα λευκότερα χιόνος,
ίππευον ίππων σκελετούς κ᾽ εκάλπαζαν αφώνως...
το δάσος έγεμε σκιών και το νεκροταφείον, (Χ)
l. 73: θρηνάς (Χ) > θρηνής (Π)
l. 74: Κ᾽ ιδέ (Χ) > Ιδέ (Π)
l. 75: Ότε η κόρη ύψωσε το ένδακρύ της βλέμμα (Χ) > Κ᾽ εν ω η κόρη ένδακρυς ανύψονε το βλέμμα (Π)

APPENDIX II
SYNOPTIC COMPARISON OF MARMIER, LE RETOUR D'UNE MÈRE ~
PARASCHOS, ΜΗΤΡΟΣ ΕΠΑΝΟΔΟΣ

X. Marmier, *Chants populaires du Nord*, Paris 1842, 108-11:

Α. Παράσχος, *Ποιήματα*, Α΄, Αθήνα 1881, 315-318:

LE RETOUR D'UNE MÈRE

ΜΗΤΡΟΣ ΕΠΑΝΟΔΟΣ
(Κατά το Δανικόν).
Μίμησις

Α΄

Dyring s'en va dans une île et épouse une belle jeune fille.

1 Σ' ένα νησί χαρούμενος
  πηγαίνει ο Κωνσταντίνος·
2 Γυναίκα παίρνει λυγερή,
  γλυκειά γαλανομμάτα.
3 Σε μια γλάστρα εζούσανε
  σα γιασεμί και κρίνος,

Ils vécurent ensemble sept ans et eurent six enfants
La mort entre dans le pays et enlève la jeune femme.

4 Κ' έξη παιδάκια ο Θεός
  τους χάρισε δροσάτα.
5 Μα γείνηκε κατάμαυρο
  Ο Χάρος χελιδόνι,
6 Και μιαν αυγή τη λυγερή
  πηγαίνει και λαβόνει.

Β΄

Dyring s'en va dans une île et épouse une autre jeune fille.
Il épouse cette jeune fille et la ramène chez lui.
Elle était méchante et haineuse.

7 Άλλη γυναίκ' απ' το νησί
  ο Κωνσταντίνος παίρνει:
8 Ήταν μαυρομάτα ώμορφη
  και σπίτι του τη φέρνει.
9 Ήταν η νύφη άπονη
  ψυχή, καρδιά στρημμένη·

Elle arrive à la porte de la maison,

10 Στη θύρα φθάνει του σπιτιού
   με κεφαλή υψωμένη...

les six enfants sont là qui pleurent.

11 Εκεί τα έξη ορφανά
   θρηνούσαν μαζωμένα·

Les petits enfants bien affligés,

12 Ήταν πολύ τα δύστυχα
   παιδάκια πικραμένα.

elle les repousse du pied.

13 Τα σπρώχνει με το πόδι της
   και μπαίνει, δεν αφίνει

Elle ne leur donne ni bière,
ni nourriture,

14 ψωμί να φάνε, το νερό
   ολίγο τους το δίνει,

et elle leur dit: Vous souffrirez la faim et la soif. Elle leur enlève leurs coussins bleus	15 Και λέγει· "πείνα θα 'χετε και δίψα·" τους σηκόνει 16 Τ' άσπρα μαξελαράκια τους, το κάταστρο σεντόνι,
et leur dit: Vous coucherez sur la paille.	17 Και λέγει· "μέσα στ' άχερα θα κοίτεσθε το βράδυ·"
Elle leur enlève leurs flambeaux de cire et leur dit: Vous resterez dans les ténèbres.	18 Τους παίρνει τα κεράκια τους και λέγει· "στο σκοτάδι 19 Θα μένετε, τα ορφανά δεν έχουν φως κανένα· 20 Πηγαίνετε τη μάνα σας να βρήτε, ξένη γέννα!"

Γ΄

Le soir, bien tard,	21 Η μέρα σαν επέρασε, το βράδυ, πολύ βράδυ,
les enfants pleurent;	22 Συμμαζωμένα τα μικρά εκλαίγαν στο σκοτάδι,
leur mère les entend sous terre.	23 Και τ' άκουσε η μάνα τους από το μαύρο χώμα, 24 Γιατί μια μάνα και νεκρή μπορεί ν' ακούση ακόμα! 25 Τα δάκρυα που έχυναν τα έρημα παιδιά της,
Elle les écoute dans son cercueil.	26 Στο φέρετρο της μπαίνανε, σταλάζαν στην καρδιά της.
- Il faut que j'aille vers mes petits enfants.	27 "Θα πάγω!" λέγει· απ' τη γη σηκόνεται η μαύρη,
Elle s'avance devant notre Seigneur	28 Και το Θεό με της στοργής το φως πηγαίνει να βρη...
et lui dit: Ne puis-je aller vers mes petits enfants?	29 "Θεέ μου, λέγει· δεν μπορώ να πάγω στα μικρά μου;" 30 Κ' εμπρός του γέρν' η κεφαλή της πεθαμμένης χάμου,
Elle pris si long-temps,	31 Και τόσο τον παρακαλεί και τόσο τον εδεήθη,
que notre Seigneur la laisse partir. - Tu reviendras au chant du coq, tu ne resteras pas plus long-temps.	32 Οπού ο εύσπλαγχνος Θεός στον πόνο της λυπήθη· 33 "Πήγαινε, είπε, κ' έρχεσαι πριν ξημερώση πάλι".

Elle se lève sur ses jambes fatiguées,	34 Στα γόνατά της η νεκρή σηκώθη αγάλι, αγάλι,
et sa tombe s'entr'ouvre.	35 Ο τάφος μισοάνοιξε μονάχος του και βγαίνει,
	36 Και στέκεται να θυμηθή ο δρόμος που πηγαίνει...
Elle s'avance vers le village, les chiens hurlent en levant la tête.	37 Κινά στη χώρα· τα σκυλιά οπίσω της ουρλιάζαν,
	38 Την κεφαλή σηκόνανε και τη νεκρή εκυττάζαν.
Elle arrive près de sa maison, sa fille aînée est à la porte.	39 Φθάνει στο σπίτι της· εκεί στη θύρ' ακουμπισμένη
	40 Την πειό μεγάλη κόρη της ευρήκε η πεθαμμένη·
- Pourquoi restes-tu là, ma chère fille?	41 - Πώς στέκεις, κόρη μου γλυκειά, της λέγει, μοναχή σου;
où sont tes frères et sœurs? Tu n'es pas ma mère;	42 Πού είν' οι αδελφούλες σου; πού ειν' οι αδελφοί σου;
	43 - Δεν είσαι συ η μανούλα μου, της είπε πικραμένα·
ma mère était belle et riante.	44 Είχα μητέρα γελαστή κι ωραία σαν κ' εμένα,
Ma mère avait les joues blanches et roses; Toi, tu es pâle, et tu ressembles à une morte.	45 Με μάγουλα τριαντάφυλλο και όψι χιονισμένη·
	46 Συ έχεις πρόσωπο χλωμό και μοιάζεις πεθαμμένη...
- Comment serais-je belle et riante? Je suis morte, et mon visage est pâle.	47 - Πώς θέλεις να 'μαι ώμορφη και γελαστή, μικρή μου,
	48 Οπού ο Χάρος κοίτεται μερόνυχτα μαζή μου;
Comment pourrais-je être blanche et rose? J'ai été dans le cercueil si long-temps.	49 Πώς να 'χω μήλο μάγουλο και όψι χιονισμένη,
	50 Που με σκεπάζει φέρετρο και τάφος με χλωμαίνει;
	Δ'
Elle entre dans la chambre, et trouve ses petits enfants	51 Μπαίνει στο δώμα των παιδιών· τα βρίσκει τα καϋμένα
avec des larmes sur les joues. Elle brosse les vêtements de l'un,	52 Στο αχερένιο στρώμα τους χλωμά και δακρυσμένα.
	53 Το ξεσχισμένο φόρεμα του πρώτου διορθόνει·

elle peigne le second, elle relève le troisième, elle console le quatrième. Le cinquième, elle le prend sur ses genoux, comme si elle voulait l'allaiter. Elle dit à sa fille aînée: Va prier Dyring de venir ici.	54 Χτενίζει ευθύς το δεύτερο, το τρίτο ανασηκόνει, 55 Χαϊδεύει τα μικρότερα και το μωρό της πιάνει, 56 Στα γόνατά της το 'βαλε ωσάν να το βυζάνη. 57 Και εις τη μεγαλείτερη γυρνώντας θυγατέρα, 58 Της λέγει· "πες του Κωνσταντή να έλθη εδώ πέρα!"
Et quand il entra dans la chambre, elle lui dit en colère: - Je t'avais laissé de la bière et du pain, et mes petits enfants ont faim. Je t'avais laissé des coussins bleus, et mes petits enfants sont sur la paille. Je t'avais laissé des flambeaux de cire,	59 Σαν ήλθ' εκείνος, η νεκρή τού λέγει θυμωμένα· 60 "Σου άφησα για τα παιδιά ψωμί, και πεινασμένα 61 Τα βρίσκω· άσπρα σ' άφησα χιονάτα μαξελάρια, 62 Και τα παιδιά μου κοίτονται απάνω στα χορτάρια·
et mes petits enfant sont dans les ténèbres. S'il faut que je reviennne, il vous en arrivera malheur.	63 Τόσα κεριά παραίτησα για να 'χουν φως το βράδυ, 64 Και τρομασμένα κοίτονται στο άγριο σκοτάδι! 65 Έχε το νου σου, Κωνσταντή!"... και της νεκρής το μάτι 66 Φωσφόρισε στα σκοτεινά κ' εστάθηκε κομμάτι...
Voilà que le coq rouge chante, les morts doivent retourner dans la terre. Voilà que le coq noir chante, les portes du ciel s'ouvrent. Voilà que le coq blanc chante, je ne puis rester plus long-temps.	67 "Οι θύρες, είπε, τ' ουρανού ανοίξανε, χαράζει· 68 Το μαύρο ορνίθι ελάλησε και τ' άσπρο με φωνάζει. 69 Να μείνω περισσότερο δεν ημπορώ..." εστάθη, 70 Τα ορφανά της κύτταξε, εστέναξε κ' εχάθη!
	Ε'
Depuis ce temps, chaque fois que Dyring et	71 Και από τότε ο Κωνσταντής κ' η μητρυιά εκείνη 72 Εδείχνανε στα έρημα παιδάκια καλωσύνη.
sa femme entendaient les chiens grogner,	73a όταν ακούγαν τα σκυλιά να κλαίνει μέσ' στο δρόμο,

ils donnaient aux enfants de la bière et du pain. Chaque fois qu'ils entendaient les chiens aboyer, ils avaient peur de la morte. Chaque fois qu'ils entendaient les chiens hurler, ils tremblaient de la voir apparaître.	73b Σηκόνουνταν με τρόμο 74 Κι άσπρο ψωμί στα ορφανά εδίναν φοβισμένοι, 75 Γιατί ετρέμαν μη φανή και πάλ' η πεθαμμένη!...

1873

PARASCHOS 1876 AND 1881

A collation of the two editions: Βύρων Β′ (1876) 117-19 (B) og Ποιήματα Α′, 1881, 315- 18 (Π) shows the following differences. Orthographic differences have not been registered. The version of B has two more scenes (one starts after l. 37, another after l. 50), that is five in all.

Under the title: Κατά το Δανικόν του Άνδερσεν (B′), Κατά το Δανικόν. Μίμησις (Π)
l. 3: ζούσανε (B) > εζούσανε (Π)
l. 3: ῳσάν (B) > σα (Π)
l. 9: όμως η νύφη ήτανε κακή (B) > Ἤτανε η νυφή άπονη ψυχή (Π)
l. 16: μαξιλαράκια (B) > μαξελαράκια (Π)
l. 16: σινδόνι (B) > σεντόνι (Π)
l. 17: εις τα άχυρα (B) > μέσα στ' άχερα (Π)
l. 23: στο μαύρο μέσα χώμα (B) > από το μαύρο χώμα (Π)
l. 25: τα δάκρυα που χύνανε (B) > τα δάκρυα που έχυναν (Π)
l. 30: εμπρός Του (B) > εμπρός του (Π)
l. 31: δεήθη (B) > εδεήθη (Π)
l. 33: Κ' είπε· "σαν κράξ' ο πετεινός οπίσω θα 'ρθης πάλι" (B) > "Πήγαινε", είπε, "κ' έρχεσαι πριν ξημερώσει πάλι".
l. 35: ο τάφος της μισάνοιξε (B) > ο τάφος μισοάνοιξε (Π)
l. 43: μάνα μου (B) > μανούλα μου (Π)
l. 44: είχα μαννούλα (B) > είχα μητέρα (Π)
l. 46: πρόσωπο νεκρού (B) > πρόσωπο χλωμό (Π)
l. 52: απάνω εις τα άχερα με μάτια δακρυσμένα (B) > στο αχερένιο στρώμα τους χλωμά και δακρυσμένα (Π)
l. 59: φθάνει εκείνος, κ' η νεκρή (B) > σαν ήλθ' εκείνος, η νεκρή (Π)
l. 61: μαξιλαράκια (B) > μαξελαράκια (Π)
l. 67-69:
    Εκεί τ' ορνίθι άρχησε στα σκοτεινά να κράζη,
    και θάρρευες πως τη νεκρή από μακριά φωνάζει.
    Τ' άκουσε κι ανατρίχιασε, εστράφηκε, εστάθη, (B)

---

* I am much indebted to Dr. Erik Dal for his kind assistance concerning translations of the Danish folk songs.

Translating into Greek from Danish 19th Century Texts

by
Aristea Papanicolaou-Christensen

My paper concerns notes and accounts written by Danes travelling in Greece in the 19th century. Some of them only visited the country briefly while others stayed for longer periods. Their aims and activities varied considerably. Danish archives - public as well as private - hold many such documents. Most are in manuscript. There are letters to family, friends or collegues, and scientific, or rather technical reports for public authorities or boards. Also, there are personal notes, travel diaries etc. The documents are abounding with observations and memories and thus represent a valuable source of information on political and social conditions in 19th century Greece. Furthermore they hold interesting information on the daily life of the Greek. Often there are sketches or photographs of ancient monuments, landscapes and people.

Translating such documents presents its own problems and pitfalls, as I shall briefly comment on in the following paragraphs.

The difficulties start with the process of locating the texts. Printed material must be sought in the libraries, and modern information technology is of great help. But when it comes to manuscripts there are no shortcuts. It is still necessary to work the traditional way and go through the material leaf by leaf and patiently. Often the manuscripts are in bad condition and not only because of their "ageing". Many letters were pierced and smoked in the efforts to prevent cholera from spreading.

The texts are usually written in Gothic letters, lean and crabbed in order to save paper. Grammar and syntax differ considerably from modern Danish. The same holds true for orthography and choice of words which was widely influenced by German.

It is important to transcribe the manuscript carefully, since the transcription forms the basis of all further work. It goes without saying that it is essential for the work and its conclusions that "Swedish" is not rendered as "Spanish" nor "missionary" as "millionaire".

As for the translation itself priority must be given to the respect for the original. The translator must translate the entire text and avoid the temptation to render it fragmentarily and supplemented with personal paraphrases.

There is no general agreement on how to render foreign names into Greek. Personally, I prefer that the names of the main characters in the text should be transsscribed in accordance with acoustic orthography (Λύτ, Χάννε), while all names, including place names, should be kept in latin (Listov, Winstrup). On the other hand, some names have existed for a long time in a recognized, Greek transcription. In such cases these transcriptions should be maintained (Χριστιανός Χάνσεν, Θεόφιλος Χάνσεν, Ερνέστος Τσίλλερ, Ερρίκος Σλήμαν).

Many years of translating Danish texts from the 19th century have taught me that the work is not done with a mere completion of the translation. The reader needs comprehensive notes providing him with the political, historical and social background for understanding the text in the best way possible.

It is of course the primary task of the translator to vitalize the texts of the 19th century for the reader of today without betraying the author of the original.

Selected translations from Danish into Greek by Aristea Papanicolaou-Christensen:

Χριστιάνα Λυτ, Μιά Δανέζα στην Αυλή του Όθωνα Athens 1981, 1988, Ερμής. (*Fra Fredensborg til Athen. Fragment af en Kvindes Liv,* Copenhagen 1926, Gyldendalske Boghandel, og *Breve fra Grækenland, Smyrna, Phokaea, Mytilene, Chios, Tschesme, Ephesus og Patmos, 1846,* af Christiane Lüth, Copenhagen 1884, J. H. Schultz).

Χριστιάνα Λυτ, Αθήνα 1847-1848, Athens 1999, Ερμής. (Det Kongelige Bibliotek, Håndskriftsafdelingen).

Χριστιάνα Λυτ, Αρμενίζοντας, πέντε ταξίδια στο 1845-1851, Athens 1999, Ερμής. (Det Kongelige Bibliotek, Håndskriftsafdelingen).

Χριστιανός Χάνσεν. Επιστολές και σχέδια από την Ελλάδα, Athens 1993, Ωκεανίδα. (Det Kongelige Bibliotek, Håndskriftsafdelingen. Rigsarkivet. Kunstakademiets Bibliotek, Samlingen af Arkitekturtegninger).

Βρένστεδ και Αλή-Πασάς, Εθνικό Ίδρυμα Ερευνών, Κέντρο Νεοελληνικών Ερευνών, Athens 1998. (*P. O. Brøndsteds Reise i Grækenland i aarene 1810-1813,* p. 242-270, København 1844).

How Danish and Greek Legal Languages Meet in the Multilingual Environment of the European Community

by
Dimitrios Papanikolaou.

There are 15 Member States in the European Union, representing 12 languages. In order to stress the particular status of these 12 languages, it should be sufficient to mention that the United Nations with approximately 150 states are represented linguistically by only 5 languages. Or that the Council of Europe, which assembles nearly all of the European countries, gives them voice in only 2 languages. The key word in the EU is "official": all 12 languages are equal in authority, all legal texts have to be issued in all these languages with the important consequence that in principle not one single language can be considered a translation target.

However, this charming picture appears under a somewhat cruder light when seen at close range.

Firstly, not all national languages have official status. This applies to Luxembourgish and, with some very rare exceptions, to Irish Gaelic.

Secondly, parallel to George Orwell's "Animal Farm", there are some languages that are more official than others, such as French, English and, not seldom, German. Here, we speak not of a Big Brother, but of Big Languages; yet the consortium of the Big 3 is not monolithic. In Brussels, French and English are spoken besides Dutch, being on the same footing as by force of things, with a slight preponderance of French, whereas in Luxembourg French clearly has the upper hand followed by German, probably because of the German character of the region, and with English only third.

If the position of the Big Ones may vary, however, the fate of the Small Ones, to whom Danish and Greek belong, remains the same, no matter whether you are in Brussels or in Luxembourg.

The above mentioned key-word "official" may be true for all the languages, but it is obvious that you cannot expect to be well served if, for instance, you ask your French usher in Danish or Greek to dispatch a letter. You have to use one of the Big Languages understood more or less by everyone. This is a crucial point in the process of recruiting staff in general and translators in particular. The large majority of the candidates who land in the Communities speak English, French or German, the foreign languages that are necessary in order to be admitted - the so to speak first class languages - not rarely accompanied by the "second class languages": Italian and Spanish and extremely seldom by Danish, Finnish, Greek and others, which are the third class languages.

Roughly seen, the third class languages have some particularities in common, but let us focus here on Danish and Greek, bearing in mind the Danish and Greek legal translator.

The Danish language belongs to the group of so-called Germanic languages. The Greek legal translator who already speaks German or English has considerable facilities learning Danish, especially as far as the vocabulary is concerned. On the other hand, however, he has to be very careful not to be caught in the trap of "faux amis" - misleading similarities - and has to get used to the specific structure of the Danish language, which is often deceiving in its apparent simplicity and conciseness. Ambiguities and equivocal expressions can be perplexing to the translator[1].

The Greek language, on the other hand, although it belongs to the family of Indoeuropean languages, only remotely presents common features with the languages of the same family and offers a great deal of difficulties to the Danish translator. There is no point of reference to other languages as far as vocabulary is concerned. Most words have to be memorised mechanically and by repeated efforts and orthography has in some cases recently been arbitrarily changed, so that research in the dic-

---

[1] Some very simple examples:" Ret" can mean law as well as tribunal or "virksomhed" can mean enterprise but also commercial activities. Please believe me, it is not as harmless as it appears: the enterprise may be legal but not its activities, and if you make a mess of it in the translation, the result will be catastrophic.

tionary becomes almost impossible to foreigners. The most serious problem is, perhaps, that there is not always a universally accepted *dimotiki*, i.e. modern spoken new Greek, but rather a *dimotiki* with a considerable number of loanwords from Katharevousa, a somewhat artificial high Greek formerly taught and spoken under official circumstances. In order to complete the picture it should be mentioned that many authors and speakers often use words or expressions deriving from the depths of the more than 4000 year old Greek language.

A very interesting illustration of these compiled difficulties is offered by the so-called feta case[2]. This case, concerning a dispute between Denmark and Greece, bore on the right alleged by the Greek government to use the name feta exclusively for the Greek product, whereas Denmark, who has been producing Danish feta since 1971, put forward that the denomination had become common to all other feta producing countries.

In an attempt to prove the exclusive Greek character of feta, the Greek government turned to Greek Mythology, claiming that cheese, as a precursor of feta presenting its features, was made by the Cyclops Polyphemos. Hesiodos was also cited. Then, passing through the Panathinea festivities, during which cheese was offered to the goddess Athina, and dwelling a bit on the Golden Age of Pericles, when feta was the official meal at public festivities, the Greek government stressed the fact that Byzantine emperors used to tax their subjects *in natura*, that is in feta.

In this case, it is interesting to see how a legal problem can take cultural dimensions. Thus, the Greek government submitted that feta is one of the features of the cultural element of Greece. Actually, words exist such as Τυρευτήρ, which means cheese producer and was one of the names of Hermes, or Τυρώ (a noble daughter famous for her whiteness and softness, like feta) or descriptions of the method of cheese making as in Rhapsody I of the Odyssey. Finally, there are some instances cited up to our time.

Roughly presented, these are the difficulties that the Danish and Greek translators are faced with and which appear in a particular perspective when dealing with legal texts.

Legal translation within the community institutions differs from other

---

[2] Feta is Greek white cheese.

kinds of translation mainly in respect of the necessity of accuracy of the contents, requiring a careful choice of terms to be used and also in respect of the legal effects attached to it, effects that must be identical with regard to all languages. It is useful to note that terminology is of dubious help in this matter. While in other fields, especially in applied sciences, a term very often has a precise meaning even if used to indicate different things, legal terms may be used with different conceptual purposes, necessitating themselves an interpretation according to the given context. In fact, legal translation has as a primary target the localisation of the intrinsic meaning of the legal term itself; the translation of the whole text afterwards does not necessarily depend on the legal quality of the translator. Naturally, legal collocations must be observed, even if the meaning remains clear, otherwise the reader would get ill predisposed to the legal competence of the translator.

Danish and Greek legal languages should normally come into contact with each other in their natural environment, which is the field of Community legislation where Community institutions pass regulations, directives, decisions etc. However, this is not the case. At least not officially. In fact, although drafts are prepared in one of the so-called working languages, usually French or English, the text that appears in the Official Journal of the European Communities is authentic. As all the languages are official, none of the texts is considered as constituting a translation.

The two languages really come into contact with each other in law fields almost exclusively in the frame of the Court of justice of the european Communities, commonly known as the European Court (hereafter "the EC"). Here, although all the languages of the Member States are official, it has been ruled that in principle the procedure before the Court takes place in one language from which most documents must be translated into all other official languages and which is the deciding one in case of ambiguity. The reason for this ruling must have been the fact that in contrast to the unilateral activity of law giving bodies, that is legislation binding the whole world in terms understood by everybody, many factors using different languages are implicated in the process of case law activity, such as parties, judges, advocate generals, representatives of Member States, etc.

There are different kinds of procedures before the EC. Seen linguistically, all these procedures have in common that once a case has been brought before the EC, it follows its course wrapped in a new linguistic overcoat, which is tailored to community measures. This point needs some explanation. It entails by no means a transfiguration of the national language. The sole effect is that the case is further treated by largely using legal terms and expressions proper to community law, which is a natural consequence of the fact that community law is independent of national law and so, accordingly, the legal language of the community institutions also has to be. Consequently, real "fresh" national language is provided only by the so-called direct actions, which are actions presented by individuals i.a. and concern situations of their national environment and, in a much larger scale, by the so-called request of national courts for preliminary rulings, where the Danish and Greek legal languages actually come into direct contact with each other as ways of expressing their genuine national environment. Here, the national court asks the Court of Justice in its own language to give an interpretation of disputed matters of community law in connection with a case pending before the national court. As already mentioned, the request written so to speak in "fresh" Danish or Greek is the only original text and is sovereignly decisive for all other languages into which it must be translated. This also explains the fact that among all the legal documents that are translated, the requests for preliminary rulings present the greatest difficulty, as it confronts the translator directly with terminology and institutions of the national legal system which he might never have heard of before.

It may be useful to point out here that if used frequently, the procedure of the preliminary ruling can to some extent entail the infiltration of national law into community law, accordingly influencing it both legally and linguistically. This has happened with German tribunals who present the highest number of requests for preliminary rulings, thus enabling the enrichment of community law and community legal terminology through German legal institutions and some times through German legal terminology[3].

---

[3] Please note that Danish and Greek tribunals are the most reluctant to submit questions to the EC.

Now, even in the frame of direct actions and preliminary rulings, the Danish and Greek languages may still see one another from a distance and not have shaken hands yet. This is quite common when there are no translators available for Greek or Danish. It is usually the case when a new team of translators is formed on the occurrence of the adherence of a new member state. As mentioned above, it is very rare that newcomers master small languages. Until the new team disposes of its own small language specialists, it will therefore have to work by means of relay translations, which usually are made from French, the de facto working language of the Court, but not seldom from English or German. Although all translations of the Court's linguistic services are very carefully made, some inconveniences are almost impossible to avoid in the case of relay translations.

The French translator, for instance, has the French lawyer in mind for whom he is translating and with whom he shares the same traditions, mentality and legal formation so that the Danish text, for instance, has to be translated accordingly. Even in an excellent translation all finesses and genuinely Danish features of the original text will be lost or, in the best of cases, replaced by closely or remotely corresponding French ones. The thus translated Danish text now comes into the hands of the Greek translator who, following the same course as his French colleague, prepares a text having the Greek lawyer in mind. The final text will be correct but there will be nothing in it that reminds of the Danish original except for some names. In other words, speaking in linguistic terms and, *ceteris paribus*, the cognitive element will have been saved, but not the emotive one. This does no harm from a practical point of view, but it does annihilate any chance of direct access to the cultural sources of the given language, that is to the psychological, social, national and historical factors that make up the identity of a nation and are mirrored in its language.

This is the appropriate place to mention the question of motivation to learn Danish or Greek.

The decision to learn a small language springs from a different motive than in the case of the universally more spread languages such as English, French, German and Spanish. The reason for learning a small language usually resides in very precise and concrete needs. In the tandem Danish-Greek, the Greek language somehow appears slightly more privileged. It has behind it the imposing background of ancient Greece and ancient Greek is taught in several schools all over Europe so that it is easier for the foreigner who has had ancient Greek at school to make the step toward new Greek if he feels like it. For the Greek, on the contrary, unless he works in the tourist industry in Rhodes, there is almost no reason to learn Danish except as out of a particular interest. Moreover, the Danish and the Greek lawyers are much less interested in learning one another's languages since the two legal systems appear to offer little scientific attraction at first sight as they are generally based on the same principles.

Nevertheless, the fact that both countries belong to the European Union has brought some interesting changes in the above scheme.

People embarking on the legal translator career arrive at the Court of Justice as well as at the legal translation services of other Community institutions already well equipped with two or three of the big languages permitting them to accomplish their duties in a satisfactory way. Nevertheless, Community institutions particularly encourage the learning of small languages in order to cover their needs for translation from those languages, especially by creating specific advantageous conditions such as intensive courses or full coverage of fees for studying the language in its natural environment.

Learning the language in the country in which it is spoken offers a great deal of advantages. Apart from the fact that you acquire the so-called "feeling of the language" much faster, you have the opportunity to visit the various institutions of the country, to attend a court hearing, briefly, to be in contact with the language around the clock thus becoming able to cope more easily with the texts to be translated once back at work.

It is a fact that 26 years after Denmark's adherence to the Community and 19 years after Greece's adherence, there is now no translation section that does not dispose of at least one person who can translate from these languages so that the Danish or the Greek lawyer can have direct access to the content of the original text through an accurate and faithful translation.

To some extent, legal language depends on the system it belongs to. Greek and Danish law do not belong to the anglo-saxon legal systems.

They are continental law systems, both influenced by Roman law - Greek law more directly than Danish law - yet keeping some proper features conditioned by their historical evolution, Danish law being part of the Scandinavian family on the one side and Greek law keeping or receiving back some genuinely Greek institutions under the cover of Roman law[4]. As long as the two languages work with the conceptual tools of their common references to Roman law, the Greek and Danish legal translators can only be happy to encounter a familiar law institution under the corresponding Greek or Danish term. But things begin to turn difficult when there is a Danish term, for instance, whose subject matter has no equivalence in the realities present in the other country or, inversely, there is a reality for which no corresponding term exists in the other country.

This might be illustrated by the example of the cases brought before the Court concerning the right of foreign teachers to work at the Greek private schools known under the name of *"Frontistirion"*. These schools do not form part of the Greek educational system but are private teaching bodies whose aim is to aid schoolboys to prepare for entering universities and high schools. The Danish translator was at his wit's end having to translate this term. The difficulties were almost insurmountable. He could not decide whether it was about schools for children with special needs or for children of poor families or whatever else and finally chose to leave the term untranslated, and with good reason: Danish schools seem to suffice by themselves in preparing people for higher education, which is not the case in Greece where the *frontistirion* acts as a parainstitution (by-institution) of the national education system[5]. The phenomenon was just unknown in Denmark and therefore impossible to be given a name, contrary to the situation where a legal term has no equivalent in the other language; here, a paraphrase might solve the problem, but how could you define a situation completely unknown to the national reader?

To conclude, I would like to underline the mere fact of the possibili-

---

[4] That is why it is sometimes called "jus grecoromanum".
[5] With, between us, very good results besides the fact that it is rather expensive.

ty of direct and immediate contact between translators of different nationalities. Your Danish or Greek neighbour may be two doors away and can within some minutes help you to get rid of a linguistic or legal problem (a contact that would be lost in the case of a relay translation), helping you decisively in this way to avoid an error that otherwise would have been committed every time your research in dictionaries and law books had not helped in the matter.

Learning Danish or Greek is a task that normally covers a period of at least three or four years before you feel able to translate without having to consult the translation already made in another language, and although the motivation is often somehow dictated, it is a fact that you are consequently familiarized with the respective country and your interest for its social and cultural events is steadily kept awake.

The result can only be positive, given the geographical remoteness and the differences in mentality and temper between the two peoples.

Eurospeak: Neologisms and Other Translatory Phenomena in Danish and Greek. The European Parliament Minutes and Reports Corpus.

by
Leo Kalovyrnas

The European Union has created a new reality at several levels. Its initial aim to constitute an economic union has expanded to include political union if not unity. Of late there is a lot of talk about Europe uniting at a military level as well, although one may safely rest assured that this is much more difficult to achieve than economic convergence, as the recent war in the Balkans has attested.

However, the European Union's success is being tested not only on the military field, but on a *linguistic* one as well. There is another war going on between the different languages that have been given official status in the EU. I am not referring to the various infamous rumours about making EU proceedings more cost-effective by dispensing with translation into all the minor languages. That may or may not happen. What is indeed happening, however, is the constant onslaught of the major languages, mainly English and French, into the territory of minor ones. The consequences of this insidious invasion are already obvious both in Danish and Greek. What needs to be stressed, however, is that this invasion is not some well thought-out, deliberate or evil plan on behalf of the countries that happen to have larger linguistic communities, but that it is happening by permission, and dare I say, invitation of the speakers of the minor languages. Speakers, yes, but more importantly, translators. But I'll come to this later.

I mentioned earlier a new reality being forged through the European Union. This new reality is also a linguistic one. In turn, this new linguistic reality affects and even shapes our cultural and social reality, the world we live in. As Pavel aptly points out[1], "... languages are not only seen as social tools that human communities have created and are continually refining for communication purposes, but also agents that constantly condition individual behaviour by virtue of social interaction in historically, geographically and culturally defined settings." That is exactly why language use in the EU and consequently translation is much more important than one may think.

Over the past thirty or so years, we have witnessed a whole new set of vocabulary being constructed to the extent that we may today safely claim that there exists an EU jargon – full with terms, turns of expression and even syntax.

This begs the question, which language or languages is this new reality being forged in originally? It is common knowledge that most EU official documents are originally written in either English or French. Then they are translated from one of these languages into the minor ones. For example, around 80% of the documents translated into Danish are originally drafted in French[2].

Thus, this new linguistic reality that is created in Brussels and Strasbourg is then translated into Greek and Danish by the EU translation services. Community translators are called upon to find words to describe new procedures, new laws, new authorities and agencies. Do they do a good job of it? Given the scant amount of time that is usually available, the results are more often than not fairly satisfactory but far from perfect, even though they are on the whole correct.

This paper will focus on this new EU linguistic reality and how it consequently becomes a new Danish or a new Greek linguistic reality – meaning how it affects our own national languages. Furthermore, based on the corpus of the European Parliament reports, I shall go into some aspects of stylistic discrepancies and other translatory problems between Danish and Greek.

---

[1] Silvia Pavel, Neology and Phraseology as Terminology in the making, in *Terminology, Applications in interdisciplinary communication,* edited by Helmi B. Sonneveld and Kurt L. Loening, John Benjamins publishing company, Amsterdam/Philadelphia, 1993.
[2] Carol Henriksen, Danske EF-oversættelser, in *Terminologie et Traduction,* no. 3/1991.

To go back to my initial argument about the quality of translated EU documents, it has to be stressed that one's aim is not only to produce a text that is correct, that is a text that contains all the necessary information and is unambiguous, but more importantly a text that can stand on a par with similar types of texts in the target language. Given the fact that a lot of EU documents are actually legislative and are not only for internal use but should be accessible to the wider public, they should also be linguistically accessible, as report 0476/98 stresses. That means that all translated documents should read as an original. As we very well know, however, this is not always the case. EU documents can be spotted a mile away and not only because of the particular jargon contained but also due to their syntax and overall style. It has already been pointed out that "… in a linguistically interesting way, a Community jargon is being created by Community translators, which overrides the boundaries of the respective languages both in structure and style…"[3]

This is perhaps more so in Danish than in Greek. Danes have been fortunate enough to have witnessed a tendency to have their legal documents written in simpler and more easily understandable form, as ruled by the Ministry of Justice 1969 guide on the simplification of legal documents. Greek legal documents can contain rather long-winded sentences and high-brow semi-katharevousa, so it is not this particular element that sets them apart from translated EU texts. Sometimes, however, even by Greek standards, EU sentences can be so long to the point of becoming incomprehensible. I cannot refrain from quoting one example:

Η τροποποίηση αυτή αφορούσε την απόδοση από τον αρμόδιο φορέα στο φορέα του τόπου κατοικίας των παροχών εις είδος από την ασφάλιση ασθενείας και μητρότητας που καταβάλλονται στους δικαιούχους συντάξεως ή προσόδων και στα μέλη της οικογενείας τους που δεν έχουν την κατοικία τους σε ένα κράτος μέλος, κατά την νομοθεσία του οποίου απολαύουν του δικαιώματος των παροχών αυτών (άρθρο 95 του κανονισμού 574/72) και στόχευε στην αντικατάσταση μιας κατ' αποκοπήν απόδοσης υπολογιζομένης βάσει του μέσου κόστους ανά οικογένεια από μια κατ' αποκοπήν απόδοση βασιζόμενη στο

---

[3] Γ. Μπαμπινιώτης, *Η Γλώσσα ως Αξία*, s. 269

μέσο κόστος ανά άτομο. Such constructions are not exceptional in EU documents.

Syntax

Apart from the syntactic aspect of long sentences, EU documents have created a syntax all of their own: reports and regulations begin in a set way: e.g. Europa-Parlamentet

> der henviser til traktaterne, særlig EF-traktatens artikel 199…
> der henviser til arbejdet…osv
> godkender vedføjede udkast til aftale, etc.

The following verb clauses are spaced by commas, while the actual verb of the main sentence may not show up till several pages later. Moreover, in between, one may even come across headings.

Another common trait is the overall tendency in both Greek and Danish translations for noun clauses; EU documents simply teem with clauses such as *de i artikel 5 nævnte bestemmelser* or *η συγχρόνως με την Πράσινη Βίβλο για τη νομοθεσία τροφίμων εγκριθείσα ανακοίνωση*. Such clauses render documents rather awkward and more difficult to understand. Clauses such as these are more common in the original languages (French and English) and possibly, translators are influenced untowardly by the original. Another reason for the increased use of nouns could be that noun clauses tend to be more impersonal, stolid and general in comparison to verb clauses which are more expressive and direct due to the tense, the person and the voice inherent in the verb. For example, clauses such as *De af medlemsstaterne udpegede organer* could be rephrased as *De organer, der er udpeget af medlemsstaterne*. Likewise, *της δημιουργίας κατάλληλων συστημάτων κατάταξης των προγραμμάτων* could be rephrased as *να δημιουργηθούν κατάλληλα συστήματα κατάταξης των προγραμμάτων* or *να δημιουργήσει κατάλληλα συστήματα κατάταξης των προγραμμάτων*, depending on whether one opts for the passive or active construction. It should be mentioned that long noun clauses are commonly used in Greek official documents too, so the Greek translators could always base their predilection for noun clauses to this fact. Nevertheless, excessive use of noun clauses often leads to incomprehensible or stylistically poor results, as one is forced to use a long string of genitives, e.g. *με την ανάγκη πρόληψης της ενδεχόμενης καταστρατήγησης των εθνικών μέτρων.*

Thus, in most cases cumbersome noun clauses could easily be turned into verb clauses, considering that in both Greek and Danish verb clauses sound more natural and contribute to less tiresome reading.

Lexicality

It is worth taking a close look at EU translations from a lexical point of view. Obviously, the new political, economic and administrative reality that is being forged calls for a new nomenclature. EU documents teem with a cornucopia of new terms. Nevertheless, these new terms have not sprung naturally out of the language corpus of each separate linguistic community in the member states – that is, they are not words coined by national speakers in a national language context - but more often than not, they are translated from one of the major languages. Care is indeed taken when it comes to rendering some of the major official terms, such as names of committees, bodies, procedures and so forth. A fairly large number of other, less official terms, however, are translated in a more off-hand manner, giving rise to several problems. The point of fact is that each translator is often left up to her own devices as to how she may translate several common new EU concepts. This entails that what we now have on our hands is a kind of polymorphism[4]– different isoglosses which create confusion as to which one is, or should be, the official one.

There are certain criteria[5], which govern whether a term is successful or problematic in its use. Terms should be characterised by 1. acceptability, meaning just how acceptable the term is to the final recipient, i.e. the language user (e.g. *semantics* is now rendered as *σημασιολογία* and not as *σημαντική*); 2. informativity, that is the informational content contained in the term, meaning its denotations, its transparency and clarity (e.g. *multimedia* is translated as *πολυμέσα*, stating exactly what it is about); 3. recallability, meaning exactly how easy a term is to recall, depending on how long it is, whether it consists of one word or several

---

[4] Oswald J. L. Szemerenyi, *Introduction to Indo-European Linguistics*, Oxford Linguistics, 1999, p. 300.
[5] Γ. Μπαμπινιώτης, *Η Γλώσσα ως Αξία*, s. 36.

and whether it is easy to use (e.g. the term *hormonforstyrrende stoffer* is translated in Greek by several words: *χημικές ουσίες που προκαλούν ενδοκρινικές διαταραχές,* and so it is neither short nor monolexical, making its repeated use in long phrases rather difficult; and finally 4. the term's translatability, which can be defined as the ease with which one may be led to the equivalent foreign term, e.g. the term *samforbrænding* corresponds well to the term *συναποτέφρωση*.

Furthermore, assessing the correctness of new terms means verifying lexico-semantic adequacy, conformity to morpho-syntactic rules (derivation, composition, abbreviation), and functionality with respect to existing terminology.Understanding the relationships between correctness, acceptability and effective communication in languages for special purposes on one hand, and the workings of linguistic creativity on the other, is important, concludes Pavel[6].

A lot of these new terms have acquired official status, so to speak, and are now considered "right", which is to say they have become standardised. As with many new terms, however, the procedure through which a term is formalised and consolidated in its use is a long and arduous one, passing through several stages of polymorphism. This means that the same term may have several translations for a long period of time until at some point, language users start favouring only one of the two, or more, variations. For example, in the eighties the word *feedback* was translated either as *ανατροφοδότηση* or *ανάδραση*, the former gradually gaining ground and now being the "proper" way of translating *feedback*. Likewise, terms such as *biodiversitet* is translated both as *βιοποικιλότητα* and *βιοποικιλομορφία,* the former gradually gain-

---

[6] "... is important for at least four reasons. It allows terminologists to recognise proper new terms from improperly formed ones and to assess their acceptability based on phraseological behaviour in thematic discourse. It allows for the co-operative dissemination of terminological information, and for its subsequent standardisation by national and international bodies. It helps language planners and terminologists, particularly comparativists, working in more than one language, develop their own lexical creativity based on assimilation of their conceptual and cultural background... Finally, it provides the means necessary for enhancing the conceptual coherence, the lexical consistency and social acceptance of terminologies-in-the- making.", Silvia Pavel, ibidem.

ing more authority. Similarly, *rationalisering* is translated as *εξορθολογισμός* and *ορθολογικοποίηση*, *frivillige aftaler* as both *εκούσιες* and *εθελούσιες συμφωνίες*, *bortskaffelse af affald* as *διάθεση* or *απόρριψη αποβλήτων*.

Another point that must be made is that the translator of specialised texts is obliged to think hard before deciding whether the author of the original text used a word or a synonym for the sake of stylistic variety or due to terminological accuracy[7]. In the examples mentioned before, is *bortskaffelse af affald* a term, thus making it obligatory to have a permanent equivalent in Greek, or is it up to the Greek translator to vary the Greek document stylistically by using *διάθεση* or *απόρριψη* interchangeably?

It cannot be stressed too much that the translator is not called upon to find a monosemic equivalent for each new concept. That is not only almost impossible but also undesirable. The same word may be used in several fields or contexts each time with a different denotation. As Babiniotis[8] points out, "what happens in terminology, is that its elements refer to and are used in specific types of texts, and may differ depending on the field or the science. This fact may cause certain difficulties but corroborates the argument that a term with specific content say in chemistry must not necessarily have the same translation in information science, where it may contain different meaning. A different type of text, another context, another form of communication may permit a different denotation".

This point is well-nigh a truism, since can it ever be possible or even desirable to understand terms outside of the contexts in which they are used: can they have an autonomous unambiguous meaning[9]? For example, the EU term *kapacitet* is sometimes rendered as *ικανότητα*

---

[7] Βασίλης Κουτσιβίτης, Ορολογικές και Μεταφραστικές Παρατηρήσεις με αφορμή το ελληνικό κείμενο της Συνθήκης ΕΟΚ, στο *Terminologie et Traduction* no. 3, 1986, s. 23.

[8] Γ. Μπαμπινιώτης, ibid.

[9] Fred Riggs, Social Science Terminology: Basic Problems and proposed Solutions, in *Terminology, Applications in interdisciplinary communication,* edited by Helmi B. Sonneveld and Kurt L. Loening, John Benjamins publishing company, Amsterdam/Philadelphia 1993.

απορρόφησης in Greek. We know that *kapacitet* can also mean *χωρητικότητα*. Our purpose as translators is not to find a univalent (monosemic) word in Greek for the original term, but to make sure that in spite of its polysemy the word is unambiguous in the target language text.

Neologisms

Another issue that translators of LSP texts are often confronted with is that of neology. Neologisms come about due to the lack of equivalent terminology in the target language, either because the concept is non-existent in that specific language or because it is a neologism also in the language of the original text. *Ombudsman* is an example of the first case, where the term already existed in Danish and equivalents had to be found in other languages. *Dumping* is an example of the second category: the term was new in English as well.

Neologisms sometimes are so effortless and natural sounding that they seem to have always been there, e.g. *σύνοδος κορυφής, χορηγία,* etc. Others are less successful. The same criteria that apply to term formation also apply to neologisms. Oddly enough, however, their success is not dependent on such objective, countable factors[10].

Community texts do not only swarm with lexical neologisms, such as *αυστηροποίηση, τομεακός, δικτυοθέσεις, παροχός,* etc, but also with newly fashioned collocations: *διαδικασία συνδιαλλαγής, στρέβλωση του ανταγωνισμού, καταχωρητής δεδομένων,* and so forth. In some cases, the original English terms have remained untrans-

---

[10] Pavel, ibid, writes: "The relationship between correctness and acceptability, and their respective impact on the moulding of new terminologies are not yet clearly understood. Many grammatically correct terms never find acceptance within a professional community while others become accepted only after a long, uphill battle.Incorrect ones may be readily accepted for no apparent reasons, and whereas some of these are as readily replaced, others become impossible to uproot from current usage. On the other hand, perfectly correct terminological creations that have been spontaneously adopted by a professional community for their originality and transparency are sometimes officially rejected by editors of specialised literature and other language workers, seemingly for lack of compliance with more common if uninspired term formation patterns. Conversely, officially recommended terms gather dust inside expensive hardcovers, while parallel neologisms flourish in spoken usage."

lated in Danish, e.g. *mainstreaming*, whereas in Greek they have been given a tentative translation, e.g. *οριζόντια ενσωμάτωση*. In other cases still, in Danish we have a neologism, as with *uddelegering*, whereas in Greek, translators have opted for a translation of the term, *μετάβαση εξουσιών, αποκέντρωση*. Neither of these two methods can claim to have blanket success, for sometimes the translation of a term is too ambiguous or unusable so that it is best to keep the original, as in the case of *dumping*.

Naturally, some of these neologisms are more successful than others. *ανοιχτότητα*, which has been proposed for *åbenhed*, has clearly failed to make the grade, as it is simply too ill-conceived and bad-sounding. *Διαφάνεια, ανοιχτός χαρακτήρας, ευρύτητα* are some of the possible options used in translations, with *διαφάνεια* being the most common and logical choice. There are cases, however, when one cannot steer clear from such obstacles, as for example when the original mentions both *åbenhed* and *gennemsigtighed*. In that case translators usually opt for *ανοιχτός χαρακτήρας* or leave *åbenhed* untranslated.

Τομεακός, some might argue sounds equally offensive as *ανοιχτότητα*, but that hasn't stopped it from gaining momentum and now featuring in quite a few community documents, where a genitive construction is too cumbersome.

Συγκρισιμότητα and *επιχειρηματολόγιο* are other EU neologisms which might get standardised. *Προσβάσιμος* and to a lesser extent its noun *προσβασιμότητα* have already started appearing in the national press, replacing, unnecessarily in some cases, *προσιτός*.

Needless to say, the suffix *–ποίηση* has its heyday in community documents. All manner of *–isations* and other terms are rendered by exceeding use of *–ποίηση*. Some of them are fairly acceptable, but others could be done away with and replaced by other more acceptable constructions. The suffix *–ποίηση* and less often its verb – *ποιώ* is a facile way of getting a word translated quickly with minimum effort, but the results are often poor or even outright ludicrous. Let it suffice to quote the word *ενδοπαραγραφοποίηση*? This nonsensical, extremely ambiguous term is merely trying to render *paragraph indentation* in Greek. Another example is the word *deregulation*, which boasts several translations in Greek, most of them either impossible to pronounce or extremely ambiguous. *Ανακανονιστικοποίηση* and *αποκανονιστικοποίηση* belong to the first category, while *απορύθμιση* [sic] is now more commonly used, although still remains rather ambiguous. In such cases, it would be much better for all concerned to opt for a periphrasis, such as *άρση των ρυθμίσηων*.

Similarly, why coin *ορθολογικοποίηση* when one can have the better sounding *εξορθολογισμός*? *Flagfremstilling* could make do with *παραγωγή νιφάδων*, or *επεξεργασία σε νιφάδες* rather than the unbearable *νιφαδοποίηση*. Monolexical terms are undoubtedly easier to use, and translators are justified in preferring them to periphrases, which fit with difficulty in long sentences already fraught with too many elements. Nevertheless, monolexicality is but one of the several criteria, which make a term acceptable or even usable, and therefore coining monolexical yet awkward neologisms should not be a blanket reaction to any translatory difficulties. "It is perfectly acceptable to borrow terms from the language in which the concepts have been created, or to render them in a target language by means of descriptive phrases for lack of a single term"[11]. Neologisms such as *βακτηριακή γαλακτωματοποίηση* (*suspension af bakterier*), *δομοστοιχειωτοποίηση* (*modularization*), or *συναστικοποίηση* (*conurbation*), may indeed be monolexical but are bereft of meaning none the less.

Style

Style is a textual parameter that often gets overlooked in EU texts, as it is considered of minor importance, compared to the urgency of getting the terms right. That is perhaps why EU documents leave rather a lot to be desired from a stylistic point of view.

Greek translations are stylistically inconsistent in a large number of ways. What we readily notice is the dual use of expressions and structures that belong either to katharevousa or demotic.

EU documents share a lot of common characteristics with legal and scientific texts, in that they both contain language for specific purposes. As a result, phenomena similar to the ones witnessed in legal and scientific translations are also extant in EU texts. «Legal translations»,

---

[11] Silvia Pavel ibid.

writes Koutsivitis, «are characterised by some common traits with other technical and scientific translations… The basic element that they share is the dichotomy between codified discourse and free discourse, that is technical terms and set phrases on one hand, and free text on the other»[12]. Similarly, EU documents offer a combination of scientific or LSP terms and of LGP free discourse[13]. Nevertheless, there is an antithesis between the accuracy of terms that is required and the leeway the translator has in using LGP.

Consequently, what we often notice in EU translations is a mixture of highbrow and lowbrow registers, as well as a combination of katharevousa and demotic. This diglossia does not only appear in syntax, where use of collocations and set phrases derived from katharevousa would be justified, as they are justified in legal documents, but also morphologically, as for example, when parallel types of verb suffixes, are used. Moreover, there is evident use of the dative case ($επί$ $τη$ $βάσει$, $οιωνεί$), drops in the stress in the genitive of adjectives ($ευλόγου$), widespread use of genitives instead of prepositional clauses in the accusative ($πέραν$ $αυτών$), and use of the second past tense instead of the present perfect ($επετεύχθη$, $απεδείχθη$).

It seems that translators haven't got it terribly clear whether the text should read as a legal document (full with syntactic and morphological elements that belong to legal demotic[14]) or as a general purpose text which merely contains some terminology and the occasional loan from

---

[12] Βασίλης Κουτσιβίτης, Η μετάφραση νομικών κειμένων, στο *Terminologie et Traduction,* No. 1, 1994 p. 330.

[13] Stathakos adds, "Scientific translations are governed by a paradoxical linguistic dualism. Essay discourse… allows translators enormous freedom as to its rendition in Greek. Usually, the language used is the current demotic, but translators reserve the right to incorporate all manner of language structures from other types of Greek, if they believe that it is necessary or simply desirable in order to make the text complete. There are no rules. The text is not prescribed but is always judged a posteriori. Conversely, scientific discourse is by default prescribed and expected to be accurate, faithful, succinct, and unequivocal."

[14] Βασίλης Κουτσιβίτης, Η μετάφραση νομικών κειμένων, στο *Terminologie et Traduction* No. 1, 1994 p. 338-339:
"…demotic legal language presents few differentiations from legal katharevousa vis-

katharevousa. Otherwise, it can't be explained how in the very same translation one comes across morphological dualities such as επετεύχθη but also αποδείχθηκε, κατάστασης and later λήξεως. Such dual use of the two language forms is not confined to grammatical suffixes but spills over into syntax and collocations, e.g. the same translation uses the katharevousa type καλεί την Επιτροπή όπως προσδώσει, but also its demotic equivalent καλεί την Επιτροπή να αναθεωρήσει, να τύχει παροχών, or again χύδην and εις ό,τι αφορά, but also χύμα and σέ ό,τι αφορά.

Likewise, Henriksen[15] has observed a similar blending of formal and informal style in Danish EU texts. For example, *Stipendier og støtte ydes i en periode, der normalt kan SVINGE fra 6 måneder til 2 år*, and later on in the same text, *Det er grunden til, at Kommissionen samtidig med, at den har forsøgt at tage hensyn til de særlige forhold i hver enkelt berørt region, HAR GIVET SIG I KAST med til en vis grad at harmonisere hovedfelterne for sin intervention*. She has also observed that translators have a predilection for periphrases for stylistic purposes, e.g. *gav udtryk for påskønnelse af* instead of *påskønnede*, *at få påført AIDS* instead of *at få AIDS*, and so forth.

Another phenomenon that is observed is the tendency to use fancier, more highbrow words and collocations when an ordinary word would do the job. E.g. translators prefer constructions such as προσδίδω προσοχή, περιέρχομαι σε ανεργία and διερευνώ instead of something much more commonly used such as δίνω προσοχή, μένω άνεργος, or even δίνω προσοχή, or ερευνώ. A report on egg-producing hens (0481/98) uses words such as κλωβός and όρνιθες, which clearly do not belong to spoken Greek and are of a totally different register to the English original which talks about *cages* and *hens*, or the Danish one which refers to *bur* and *høns*. As a result, Greek translations are often of a higher register. This is corroborated by other research in this field[16] which attests

---

à-vis vocabulary, and certainly palpably fewer when compared to koine modern Greek; it also presents parallel morpho-syntactic divergence from the spoken language system and convergence with older and more scholarly stages of our language."

[15] Carol Henriksen, Danske EF-oversættelser, Hvordan ser de ud, set med danske øjne? Og hvorfor ser de ud som de gør? in *Terminologie et Traduction*, No 3, 1991.

[16] Christina Kalyviotou, Σύγκριση του ελληνικού και αγγλικού κειμένου της

to the use of a higher register in Greek translations which does not correspond to the English original. For example the Greek translation chooses ευρίσκεται for *is located*, ευλόγου for *reasonable* and εσφαλμένων for *any*.

The coining of new collocations, all non-existent in the national language corpus is also a frequent characteristic of EU jargon. Examples of that would be, *υιοθετώ θετικές δραστηριότητες, οριζόντια επισήμανση, ζητώ αντιδράσεις*. As Koutsovitis has already pointed out, the Greek language is affected grammatically too due to the influence of EU jargon. Words which never had a plural form in Greek may now boast one. Naturally, these new plural forms are not confined to EU jargon but spill over into the national language corpus, since EU documents have a regulatory or legal role. Besides, these same words are used by politicians, members of the European Parliament and so forth. Thus, Greek has now been enriched with words such as *πρόοδοι* and *δράσεις*.

Part of the problem with new collocations is that "as far as established terms are concerned, specialised vocabularies designed for translators still consist mostly of nouns and noun phrases from which verbs and verb phrases are conspicuously absent. As for LSP phraseology, i.e. the interphrasal combinations of terms and words in actual LSP discourse, it is at best given cursory consideration. More often than not, it is completely ignored on the mistaken assumption that LSP collocations are not unlike common language ones"[17].

Conclusion

Pavel[18] seems to put the argument in a nutshell: "Part of the problem seems to lie with the borderline of what constitutes effective communication, and with the power of their advocates to effectively impose one view at the expense of another regardless of the situational variables of LSP discourse. For those who believe that language only exists as an instrument, communication is effective to the degree that it is lexically stereotyped and syntactically simplified. In such a minimalist view, fig-

---

κοινοτικής οδηγίας 97/36 ΕΚ, εργασία για το μεταπτυχιακό τμήμα μεταφρασεολογίας του Ιόνιου Πανεπιστημίου 1999.

[17] Pavel, ibid.
[18] Pavel, ibid.

urative language, idiomaticity and analogy should be eliminated from L-SP writing in favour of a reduced syntax, a conventional vocabulary and an unequivocal definition of concepts. For those who are aware that language shapes even as it articulates thought, effective communication means clarity of message and forceful exposition of ideas by all means available, figurative language, idiomaticity, and analogy included."

If we accept the latter definition, and personally I do, then EU translators should rethink the methodology they follow, which is based on stolid legal language and which in certain text types is out of place in the EU. Conversely, they might benefit from focusing more on the target language result, making sure that their work reads smoothly and naturally in their national language, to use another EU term.

Translation from Modern Greek into Danish at the EU institutions

by
Niels Jæger

According to Council Regulation No. 1 of 1958 (as amended upon the accession of each new Member State) the working languages of the EU institutions are the official languages of the European Union[1], which means that legally there is no distinction between official and working languages. Evidently, a language based on 5 or 10 million native speakers does not have the same function in everyday practice as one based on 90 million or as the English and French languages that are special inasmuch as they are a priori international vehicles.

Of the three main players in the EU legislative procedure, the Council and the Commission produce only very few texts in the minor official EU languages (e.g. in Greek and Danish). The experts and Member State officials that form the many committees under these two institutions usually write in one of the de facto working languages: French or English. Administrative documents produced internally within the two institutions by the EU's own officials are almost entirely in French/English. This is partly due to the fact that most texts are to be approved by a superior who cannot be expected to know all the 11 official languages, but only French and/or English in addition to his or her native language.

In 1997 the percentages of Greek and Danish as source languages were 1.1% and 0.7% respectively of the total input for translation at the

---

[1] A multilingual community at work, The European Commission's Translation Service, European Communities 1999, p. 5.
EEC Council: Regulation No 1 determining the languages to be used by the European Economic Community.
Official Journal 017, 06/10/1958, p. 0385 - 0386.
English special edition...: Series-I (52-58) p. 59.

Commission (French: 40.4% and English 45.3%), of which a considerable proportion may only have been translated into French or English. In 1997, the output percentages fluctuated around 12% of the total output for German, French and English, and between 7.4% (Swedish) and 8.7% (Italian) for the rest[2].

Translation from minor official languages, like Greek and Danish, predominately takes place at the third main player in the EU legislative process: the European Parliament (EP) and at the two consultative EU bodies: the Economic and Social Committee (ESC) and the Committee of the Regions (COR). The members of these three institutions are elected to represent the interests of important groups in the Member States. They mostly write in their native languages because knowledge of French or English is not a precondition for their election or designation. The members of the European Parliament are politicians elected by direct elections in the 15 Member States. The ESC members are representatives of civil society in the Member States (representatives from management and labour etc.), the COR members are representatives of local and regional authorities in the Member States.

Input in Greek, Danish or other minor languages is restricted to certain text types:

at the European Parliament predominantly to resolutions, petitions (complaints from EU citizens about administrative obstacles etc. at EU level), questions from members of the European Parliament to the Commission or the Council about relevant EU topics and, most important of all, reports (containing a legislative decision, amendments to a proposal from the Commission and an explanatory statement) prepared by, for example, a Greek rapporteur within the framework of the EU legislative procedure. Also letters, legal documents etc. originating in the Member States may be written in one of the minor languages.

The most important type of document produced by the ESC and the COR is the opinion. In their opinions the two committees express their views on proposals from the Commission in the framework of a consultative procedure specified in the Treaty establishing the European

---

[2] A multilingual community at work, The European Commission's Translation Service, European Communities 1999, p. 11.

Community. In addition, the Treaty allows the two committees to issue own-initiative opinions about any subject they find relevant. A member takes on the preparation of the opinion as rapporteur. The rapporteur normally writes the opinion in his/her own language.

As at the Council and the Commission, internal administrative documents (agendas, minutes of meetings, internal letters etc.) are seldom written in languages other than French or English.

In principle, the translation process at the EU institutions is the same for all language combinations.

Employment as an EU translator requires a university degree and a thorough knowledge of at least two EU languages besides the mother tongue. This is due to the fact that the general vocabulary of the texts may contain all stylistic levels, e.g. dialect, archaic forms, jargon etc. The language used by the members of the representative EU bodies may be coloured by national political or administrative usage.

As a rule translators of the EU institutions only translate into their mother tongue. It may, however, be difficult for the translation divisions of the smaller Member States to find translators that meet all these conditions. Therefore, translation departments of the minor languages sometimes deviate from the mother tongue principle in order to cover translation from other small languages and/or they use the main working languages (French/English) as "relay languages".

Finding reference material and looking up terminology is one of the most important elements of the translation work. When the references are not given in the original, which is often the case, this part of the translation work may be very time consuming.

As mentioned above the subject of the reports of the European Parliament and the opinions of the ESC and the COR is in general a communication or a proposal for legislation from the Commission. This basic document will have been produced in French (or English) and subsequently translated into the other official languages at the Commission. The rapporteurs of the European Parliament, the Committee of the Regions or the Economic and Social Committee make frequent use of the terminology and content of the basic document. Moreover, they often refer to or cite earlier texts from their own or other EU institutions discussing the same or a similar topic.

Lastly, the rapporteurs may draw on external documents such as international conventions, research documents etc.

The reference finding/terminology part of translation work is becoming more and more computerised. The Commission puts its documents into a data base (CELEX) which can be accessed directly or through the Internet by the other EU institutions. The main institutions maintain huge terminology data bases which can be consulted through the Internet. Specially developed search programmes give quick access to former documents from the translators' own institution. A detailed set of search criteria is available to the translators. The most powerful feature is the ability to search for any sequence of strings in a given language, find the texts in the source language and finally get the equivalent text in the target language. These tools not only improve the accuracy of terminology and help to find hidden quotations, but also promote consistency of the translation work in general.

If translators fail to find information in EU databases the Internet and Internet search engines will often be the last resort.

Most text types follow certain standards of layout and wording. For instance, an opinion issued by the Committee of the Regions will contain a preamble referring to the basic document of the Commission, explaining the procedure chosen, giving the name of the rapporteur and the date when the opinion was adopted by the Committee etc. The format of the front page of an opinion offers little variation and an opinion is divided into standard headings: introduction, general comments, specific comments and conclusions. The last page will always contain the signatures of the president and the secretary-general of the Committee, a date and an indication of the place where the opinion was adopted.

The EU has developed its own jargon, essentially French in origin, since French has been the internal administrative language of the Community for decades. EU concepts are first discussed and described in French (or nowadays perhaps English). EU jargon is taken over by translators and journalists working in Brussels and thus "Eurospeak" may gradually find its way into the national languages. To Danes, word by word translations are sometimes hard to understand or even misleading. The Greeks seem less reluctant to accept loan translations. Greece has a long tradition for loan translations of French administrative and legal terminology going back to the 1830s when the establishment of Greece as a modern European nation began.

In French, and in many other languages, "Europe" and the adjective "européen" are used to refer to "the EU" without giving a second thought to the fact that the EU as an administrative unit is only a part of the geographical area of Europe.

With the Maastricht Treaty and the introduction of the principles of subsidiarity and proportionality an expression like "dimension européenne" (European dimension), which is translated word by word into "ευροπαϊκή διάσταση" in Greek as well as "europæisk dimension" in Danish has become common. According to the subsidiarity principle, EU measures are only justified if they add something extra to national measures. This notion is often expressed as "valeur ajouté" (Eng.: added value), which becomes "προστιθέμενη αξία" in Greek and (occasionally) "merværdi" in Danish, but since "merværdi" is almost exclusively used in the context of taxes (VAT) in standard Danish, translators translating into Danish will normally make an effort to put it in another way (e.g by "ekstra gevinst/fordel").

Another common combination of words is "économique et social" (economic and social), which is often used in notional opposition to "politique" (political).

The EU spends money on restructuring and establishes infrastructure etc. in the poorer parts of the EU in pursuit of "cohésion économique et sociale" (economic and social cohesion), which in the Treaty has been translated directly as "οικονομική και κοινωνική συνοχή" in Greek and "økonomisk og social samhørighed" in Danish.

EU texts often refer to "milieux économiques et sociaux"("economic and social sector" or "economic and social interest groups"), which Greeks seem to accept as "οικονομικοί και κοινωνικοί κύκλοι" or "οικονομικοί και κοινωνικοί φορείς". A loan translation would however be difficult to understand in Danish. Therefore, depending on the context, Danish translators choose between one of several translations to make the content comprehensible to Danes: "interesseorganisationer", "erhvervs- og fagorganisationerne", "erhvervskredse", "organisationskredse", "arbejdsmarkedets parter" etc.

A translator translating between Greek and Danish will have to be aware of such loan translations from French and of the different attitudes the source and target languages assume regarding such expressions.

Conclusions:

Within the EU institutions Greek, Danish and other minor EU languages are used as working languages by members of the three representative bodies: the European Parliament, the Economic and Social Committee and the Committee of the Regions. EU officials and national officials meeting in an EU context use French or English.

Original texts in Greek or Danish are limited to texts produced by the members of the representative bodies and texts coming directly from Greece or Denmark.

Originals in Greek or Danish produced by the members of the representative EU bodies are heavily influenced by the fact that the basic discussions within the Commission and the Council, and the basic documents produced by these two institutions are limited to French (or English).

Texts, Translation and Subtitling – in Theory, and in Denmark

by
Henrik Gottlieb

Part I: TEXTS AND TRANSLATION TYPES
1. General outline
The aim of this paper is to focus systematically on the many faces of translation, (part I), and to give special attention to one of these faces, familiar to Greeks and Danes alike: subtitling (parts II and III).

However, before embarking on a cruise through the archipelagos of translation, the notions of 'text' and 'translation' need to be defined.

1.1 Defining Text
In everyday language, the word 'text' refers to written matter only, as opposed to either oral or non-verbal communication. In a more scholarly context, such a definition is clearly too narrow; the concept of 'text' must include all kinds of communication containing verbal signs. Accordingly, I will define the term 'text' as *any message containing verbal material*.

By this definition, a novel is a text, as is any sound film containing dialogue, or any silent film with intertitles. Likewise, a lecture or a sermon is a text, in which the words said, the way these words are said, and the body language of the speaker all contribute to the totality of expression. The 'text' of spoken discourse, then, is not simply the wording as transcribed; it includes the context in which these words are uttered.

This basic contextual – or pragmatic – approach means that when looking at a picture of, say, an American park bench with the sign "Wet paint" on it, the text *is* the totality 'picture of a bench with a sign on it'[1].

---

[1] A Danish translation of this text would be a picture of a Danish park bench with the

A picture of the bench without the sign would no longer be a text, since it is devoid of verbal content.

1.2 Defining Translation

By the term 'translation' I refer to *any process, or product of it, in which a text is transferred from one speech community to another, and where verbal elements are replaced by other verbal elements.*

According to this definition, translation covers highly diverse phenomena, including the process of rendering a French menu in Chinese, the task of the philologist who produces a French version of the Dead Sea scrolls, an American dime novel published in Mexico, a Hindi version of a Japanese computer manual, and a Danish film with Greek subtitles.

By this definition, however, activities as for instance the transfer of verbal messages into international pictograms, e.g. non-smoking signs or traffic signs, do not qualify as translations. Neither do phenomena like interpreter-mediated communication between, say, (deaf) American Sign Language users and users of British Sign Language.

Translation, then, encompasses two interlingual entities:
A) the *activities* of translating written texts, interpreting[2] oral discourse, subtitling or post-synchronizing (= dubbing) audiovisual material, etc.
B) the *results of these activities*: the literary or business translator's written works, the interpreter's oral performance, the subtitled or dubbed product, etc.

---

sign 'Nymalet' (= just painted). Translating the American sign word-by-word – into 'våd maling' – would not be pragmatically acceptable. That is simply not what you find on Danish newly painted objects. Our inclusive definition of 'text' facilitates an 'idiomatic' stance to translation; in discussing actual translations, it leads us to asking "Is this how 'similar' target culture speakers would express themselves in a similar context?".

[2] This term is used for both the process of translating speech into speech, and the product 'speech which is a translation of speech'. We refrain from using the confusing term 'interpretation' in this context, and reserve this for 'personal reasoning about the meaning of something' (in Danish *fortolkning*, as opposed to 'interpreting' = *tolkning*).

2. A typology of source texts

Different types of translation are bred by different types of text, so before discussing and comparing translations, we must take a look at the different types of sources to be translated. To this end, a number of source-defining factors will have to be identified. A listing of such 'source text parameters' is provided below. This list is not claimed to be exhaustive, only a compilation of filters, the total effect of which is to define the text types at hand. Using these filters, one will get a pretty exact multi-dimensional picture of any text (in the extended sense, as defined above). Apart from its possible usefulness for intracultural studies (literary and semiotic studies, etc.) the picture thus obtained may serve as a valuable tool for assessing the technical, communicative and receptive potentials of a translation of the text in question.

All source text parameters are relevant to all text types; there are no verbal sources of any kind that cannot be defined within these parameters.

The distinctive effect of each of the twelve parameters in the table is illustrated by a set of text type examples that only differ in respect to the parameter in question:

Source text parameters	Examples
1. Factuality Falsifiable / Non-falsifiable text	Memoirs / Novel
2. Function Informative > Persuasive > Entertaining	Street map of Athens > Billboard advertisement > Cartoon
3. Authority Normative / Non-normative	The Koran / *Arabian Nights*
4. Actual age of text Recent > > Aged > Classical	Contemporary drama > Play by Ibsen > Tragedy by Sophocles
5. Setting Familiar > Exotic	English joke > Japanese joke
6. Linguistic conventions Shared > Culture-specific	Dialogue in US drama > US action films
7. Text life Permanent > Temporary	Poetry > Brief news items

8. Semiotic texture	
Monosemiotic (simple)	*Catch 22*: The novel
/ Polysemiotic (complex)	/ The film
9. Language mode	
Spoken / Written	Lecture on Freud / Paper on Freud
10. Rhythm of reception	
Real-time / Audience-defined	Film / Book
11. Author identity	
Known	Donald Duck story by Carl Barks
/ Unknown	/ Uncredited Duck story
12. Audience	
Private > Public	Business letter > Junk mail

As is true of the *transfer parameters* discussed later, all *source text parameters* (except no. 2) are one-dimensional, displaying either binary opposition between two entities (as shown by a slash: /) or a gradual transition from one pole to another (marked by a >). Thus, a source text may have a *more or less* permanent life (see parameter no. 7), while the statements of the text in question are *either* falsifiable *or* non-falsifiable (source text parameter no. 1).

2.1 Explaining the source text parameters and the examples used

1. Factuality – or falsifiability, to be exact – is a crucial text definer, even recognized by bookstore owners and libraries in their distinction between fiction and non-fiction. The difference between these two categories is that while authors of memoirs and producers of TV documentaries should be accountable for what is claimed in their works, novelists and feature film makers are allowed to spin yarns. However, in some sense a certain novel may be closer to the 'truth' than somebody's memoirs. Still, by having chosen the fictional form of the text type 'novel', the author is beyond reproach as to the truthfulness of the events and statements contained therein – the exception being cases where, by accident, authors of novels operating on a factual frame manage to misrepresent important elements. If, for instance, a novelist changes the outbreak of the Second World War to 1936, he is no longer covered by poetic license. Fictional castles cannot always be built on sand.
2. The parameter of text function is special because it occupies a two-

dimensional field inside a triangle:

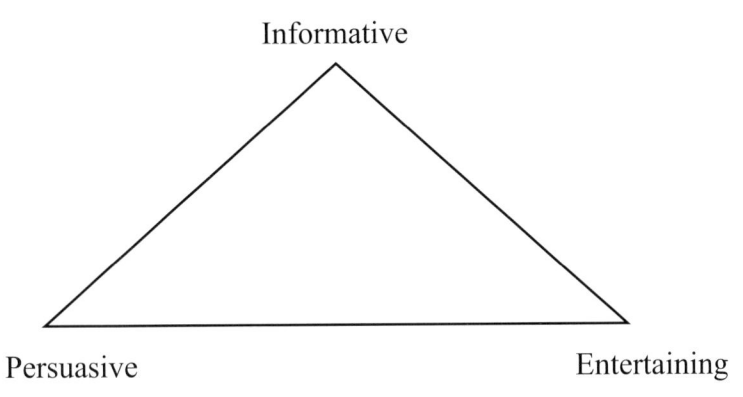

                            Informative

Persuasive   Entertaining

Most texts will belong in one of the three prototypical corners. The three examples chosen here all combine images and writing, but differ in their intended function: while a street map gives you information, an advertisement tries to persuade you to buy – or think favorably of – a certain product or company. Finally, a political cartoon (for example in a morning paper) is there to entertain you – and to break the monotony of the columns on the printed page. Of course, commercial texts are not the only persuasive texts around; religious and political materials share this function by urging people to believe or act in certain ways.

3. The authority parameter deals with the status of the text. In this respect, normative texts, e.g. legal documents and religious scriptures, are contrasted by texts with no implicit normative power. Whereas the latter types may give the translator considerable leeway in interpretation, legal and religious documents offer fewer degrees of freedom. If, for instance, a text is supposed to possess divine provenance and authority, the strategies available to the translator may differ fundamentally from those used when dealing with a strictly mundane source (cf. transfer parameter 1, below). The two best-known classic Arabic texts worldwide, *Arabian Nights* and the Koran, differ mainly in this respect, the former – a series of mundane stories – often abridged or otherwise changed in translation; the latter, with its canonical status within Islam, 'respectfully' translated throughout the centuries, if translated at all.

4. The actual age of a text about to be translated is one of the 'soft' pa-

rameters, as texts from previous periods may be – but do not have to be – treated differently than present-day works. Classical drama, for instance, has more translational options open to it than contemporary plays, as different dramatic devices, including the language, may or may not be updated – as is regularly seen in modern Shakespeare productions.

5. The setting of a text, in time and space, may also define what happens in translation. In certain types of text, for example the genre of jokes, a setting which is alien to the target audience – as in the case of a Japanese 'domestic' joke – may be modified in translation, whereas references to phenomena known in the target culture – as found in the English joke – will most often be maintained in a translation into, say, Danish.

6. Similarly, the linguistic conventions of a text constitute a relevant parameter, as the style may be changed in translation, especially if the source text belongs to a genre or culture perceived as 'exotic' in the target culture. Thus, the heavy slang in American action movies is often toned down when these films are screened or broadcast in Eastern and Southern Europe, whereas the more urbane language in American drama is replaced by language of the same stylistic quality as that of the original dialogue.

7. The parameter of expected text life is linked with what is traditionally labeled 'literary quality'. In sorting various texts according to their status as either permanent or temporary, one would place most factual texts and 'mediocre' – not to mention 'poor' – fiction close to the *temporary* end of the scale, while 'quality' fiction and a few non-fiction classics would be considered of permanent value. New items – no matter their quality – will be very short-lived, while good poetry, though hardly best-selling, may count on a rather long life span, and thus have a greater chance of being (re)translated at some later stage.

8. As for semiotic texture, simple text types (using verbal material only) form a very different basis for translation than the more complex ones, where the content of non-verbal channels has to be taken into account in translation. In the example chosen here, the novel in question tells the same story as the film based on that novel. But what is expressed monosemiotically in a novel, solely through writing, oc-

cupies four channels in a film: dialogue, music & effects, picture, and – for a smaller part – writing (displays and captions, plus in a few original films, even subtitles). A screen adaptation[3] of a 100,000 word novel may keep only 20,000 words for the dialogue, leaving the semantic load of the remaining 80,000 words to the non-verbal semiotic channels – or to deletion.

9. The language mode in question is of utmost importance. Whether the message to be translated is spoken or written (no matter the translation mode, cf. transfer parameter 8) to a large extent defines the interpretation of the text at hand. Thus, a lecture not based on a script will differ considerably from an essay on the same subject written by the same speaker, simply because the cognitive processes of speaking and writing are different: the immediacy and implicitness of speech contrasts with the planning and explicitness of writing. Some polysemiotic texts are 'bimodal' in that they use both oral and written signs (see point 8 above) but the large majority of texts to be translated include either speech or writing, not both.

10. From a certain perspective, the rhythm of reception parameter runs parallel to the parameter of language mode just covered. Most written text types can be read at any speed the individual reader may settle for, and even discontinuous reading is possible (reading the last pages of a novel before deciding whether to bother with the whole book is a usual strategy for some people). This audience-defined rhythm of reception is not possible in spoken discourse, be that natural conversation, radio announcements or film dialogue. Even some types of writing fall into this 'transient' category, such as certain computer prompts, internet ads and captions in films and on TV.

11. Knowledge of author identity cannot always be taken for granted, and the author persona – or anonymity – of a text will usually have

---

[3] Adapting a novel for stage or film purposes is an example of a type of transfer *not* dealt with in this paper. The *intersemiotic*, but not *interlingual*, process of converting a strictly verbal 'original' into a polysemiotic text – in which most of what was verbal is transformed into nonverbal visual or auditive signs – does not conform with our initial definition of 'translation'. (For a discussion of intersemiotic translation vs. interlingual and intralingual translation, see Jakobson 1966 and Gottlieb 1994, 55).

an effect on the way that text is translated. As an example of this, the now-famous creator of Duckburg, Carl Barks, may have his Disney comics (re)translated more reverently now than when he was only a nameless cartoonist on the Disney payroll in the middle of the last century.

12. Whether the audience is private or public, i.e. known to the sender or not, is another factor influencing the way texts are translated. A text created with one specific source-language recipient in mind will, when translated, function more as a citation or documentation than as a text in its own right. This would not happen with a translation of a less 'private' text. In this way, while a Danish translation of a personal German business letter would not function as a business letter in Denmark, a (freely) translated piece of German commercial junk mail, with the addressee changed, might still serve its purpose.

3. A typology of translation

In addition to this examination of the potential impact of source-text features on translation, we shall now discuss the features of translation itself.

Looking at the parameters presented in the table overleaf, we find that – as was the case with the source text parameters earlier – some parameters display an either-or opposition, (e.g. no. 3) while others establish a continuum between two extremes, such as no. 9. Finally, transfer parameter no. 7, referring to text volume, presents plus-minus deviations from a default value.

Transfer parameters	Examples
1. Purpose of translation	
Identical	Old Testament as pre-Christian tales
/ Altered text function	Old Testament as part of Christian church Bible
2. Direction of transfer	
Into translator's native tongue	Eco into Danish by a Dane
/ From translator's native tongue	/ Høeg into Italian by a Dane
3. Directness of transfer	
Direct / Relay translation	Subtitling into Danish from Greek / Via English

4. Working basis
Source text only /   Translation of new text
Existing domestic translation(s)   / New translation of classic text

5. Translator's responsibilties
The entire translation process / Verbal phrasing only   TV / Cinema subtitling

6. Preparation
Pre-produced   Time-cued subtitling (taped)
/ Impromptu   / Simultaneous subtitling (live)

7. Verbal volume of translation
Extended > Complete   Annotated volume > EU legal text
> Condensed > Summarized   > Subtitle > Abstract

8. Semiotic fidelity
Isosemiotic (language mode retained)   Dubbing
/ Diasemiotic (language mode altered)   / Subtitling

9. Co-occurrence of original
All semiotic channels present   Surtitled Greek stage play[4]
> Some channels present   > Dubbed Greek film
> No part of original present   > Printed translation of the Iliad

10. Status as translation
Manifest (translator credited)   Adventure movies
/ Concealed (translator not credited)   / Adventure computer games
/ Invented (no original exists)   / 'Exotic' stories

11. Verbal translator-audience two-way communication
Impossible > Necessary   Conference > Community interpreting

12. Diversification
Individual / Mass reception   Optional subtitles / Standard subtitles

---

[4] As opposed to subtitling, surtitling is used in foreign-language stage performances, typically drama and opera. In surtitling, the surtitles are projected onto the proscenium above the stage in order to be visible to the entire audience. As no consecutive performances of the same play have exactly the same duration, all surtitles have to be cued in real time, often by a stage technician.

3.1 Explaining the transfer parameters and the examples used

As was the case with the source parameters, all transfer parameters apply to all text types, although few translators will meet them all in their professional lives. But in a scholarly context, we are limited neither by what types of assignments we are likely to get as practising translators, nor by what types of texts we personally prefer to read, watch or listen to.

1. As a rule, the purpose of a translated text is identical with that of the original. But sometimes, a functionally different translation of a text is desired. Especially persuasive texts are prone to serving new purposes. Some texts need not even be 'changed' in translation to do this: the best way to ridicule dictators in foreign lands is often to translate their propaganda verbatim. The example used for this parameter is another persuasive text genre, religious literature. The question of what purpose to have in mind when translating Biblical material still exists, even in a society as secularized as Denmark. This was revealed a few years ago in the heated debate on the Christological manipulations in the official Danish 1992 translation of the Old Testament[5].

2. Among Western language professionals, it is almost undisputed that translators should work from a foreign language into their mother tongue. However, at many universities and similar institutions, students are still taught 'reverse' translation, that is, translation into a language of which they are not native speakers. And in several minor speech communities, Finland and Slovenia, for instance, it is deemed necessary to make do with local translators in a number of situations where the direction of transfer is *from* the domestic language, not into it. Looking at our example, to some Italian-speaking Danes it may seem easier to translate Peter Høeg's rather clinical language into Italian than to render Umberto Eco's intricate web of words in Danish. Nevertheless, judged by an Italian, the fluency of Høeg's text may suffer severely when translated by a Dane.

3. Normally, the translator will work directly from the source language

---

[5] This debate was launched by the students' magazine *Faklen* in the autumn of 1996 (Pedersen Herbener & Engelbreth Larsen 1996a & 1996b) and went on for months in the Danish printed news media.

into the target language, but for example with literature from so-called lesser-used languages, the directness of transfer is less simple. What typically happens is that not until a novel in, say, Yoruba is translated into English or French does it stand a chance of being translated into languages as for instance Greek and Danish – with the (English) relay version serving as a surrogate original in that process. However, in satellite-transmitted television, broadcast simultaneously with subtitles in a number of languages, English does not often function as a relay – or pivot – language between source and target languages; English *is* the source language in most cases. Here, the program is first subtitled into, for example, Swedish. In this process, the Swedish subtitler downloads the exact timing of all subtitles on the disk[6]. Using this disk as a shortcut to new language versions, subtitlers in the other speech communities involved – Denmark and Norway, for instance – only have to retranslate the words on the disk; no technical work needs to be done. Results are not always brilliant, though, as we will see in section 5.2, discussing pivot subtitling from Greek.

4. Moving from a situation where the translator may find the original replaced or supplemented by surrogate versions, we shall now examine the situation when a supplementary working basis may already be available in the target language. In other words, it makes a difference whether the translator is the first person to translate a new source text, or whether he or she carries on a tradition of retranslating the classics of Homer, Hugo, Dostoyevski or Dickens, to mention a few. In Denmark we recently witnessed a special case, in which two translations of the same classic (Cervantes' *El Ingenioso Hidalgo Don Quixote de la Mancha* from 1676-77) were launched almost simultaneously, by two competing publishers. While the two volumes of a more "philological" translation, by Rigmor Kappel Schmidt, was published by Centrum in 1998 and 1999, a more "contemporary" one-volume version was published by Rosinante in 1999, translated by Iben Hasselbalch[7].

---

[6] For a discussion of the technical processes of subtitling, see Gottlieb 1994 and Ivarsson & Carroll 1998.

[7] Cf. the preface of a recent study of the two Danish versions of a novel by the Nobel prize-winning Spanish author Camilo José Cela (Flintholm 1998).

5. The parameter referring to the translator's responsibilities has special relevance to polysemiotic text types. But even in written translation, it makes a difference whether the translator is trusted with the layout of the final product, or this is left to others. As for film, video and TV, it makes a major difference whether – as in the case of dubbing and cinema subtitling – only the strictly verbal transfer is done by the translator, or whether he or she creates a complete target-language version, technically integrating the new verbal material with the non-verbal tracks of the original product. In most subtitling countries, TV translators perform all subtitling functions, including the time-cueing of each title, securing optimal linguistic and esthetic results.
6. Concerning preparation, interpreters used to be the only translators working in 'real time', i.e. without having access to the entire source text before translating it. In recent years, however, a new type of translation, also lacking time for preparation, has emerged: *simultaneous subtitling*. As with 'simultaneous' interpreting, there is no synchrony between the original spoken discourse and the translation, but a time lag of at least four seconds, which partly ruins the viewer's chance of linking the words on the screen to the right speaker, who may not be visible any more[8]. Traditional interlingual subtitling remains synchronous; translators have had ample time to prepare their subtitled versions, as TV programs are seldom live transmissions. However, the subtitles for foreign items in news programs – although phrased in due time before transmission – are often exposed on the screen 'live', by the subtitler. Thus, delays of about one third of a second are common in subtitled news programs. In the field of book translation, due to market demands, translators are sometimes forced to work from non-final scripts, thus producing a series of discrepancies between published revised originals and 'original' translations.
7. As for the verbal volume of the translation, the normal state of affairs (reflecting a classical ideal) is a 'complete' rendition of the original verbal content, and this 'completeness' of a translation is indeed an

---

[8] Although in most cases, simultaneous subtitling is aimed at deaf and hard-of-hearing audiences, it does qualify as (interlingual) translation: in the Netherlands, e.g. President Clinton's testimony in the Lewinsky case was subtitled live in Dutch. (Karamitroglou 1999)

important element when evaluating literary translation quality. However, some translated novels fall far from this ideal, a Danish example being John Grisham's *The Firm (Firmaets mand)*, translated – and compressed – in 1993. Looking at non-literary text types, norms as well as practices are often different, one extreme being scholarly translations of e.g. written documents from a bygone culture. Such annotated translations may include many philological or encyclopedic notes and comments, often increasing the verbal volume considerably. At the other extreme one finds texts like the abstract of a political proposition. Although the volume may be reduced by up to ninety percent, I would consider such a text a translation, as long as essential source-language elements are adequately represented.

8. As far as semiotic fidelity is concerned, the 'default value' in translation is not found somewhere between the extremes of a continuum, but can be identified as one member of a binary pair: isosemiotic vs. diasemiotic translation. 'Normal' translation is isosemiotic: speech is rendered by speech, and writing by writing. With polysemiotic texts, this is what happens when comic books are translated, and when films are dubbed, but subtitling is different. Instead of retaining the oral language mode and thus keeping the semiotic balance of the original, subtitling shifts this balance by placing written chunks of text – exposed for between two and seven seconds each – on top of the already complex flow of dialogue, sound and images. Naturally, this additive nature of subtitling changes the working strategies of the translator as well as viewers' strategies of reception, vis-à-vis dubbing.

9. In the translated versions of polysemiotic texts – typically those found in electronic media – one finds total or partial co-occurrence of the original. Here the translation is *overt*; the audience is likely to realize that they are not confronted with the original. Total co-occurrence is found when sur- or subtitles are added to the original, or when collections of translated poems present the originals as well. Partial co-occurrence, a more common situation, can be found in e.g. dubbing and comic book translations, in which the visuals remain intact. Finally, no co-occurrence is found in the translation of all monosemiotic works, ranging from short stories to radio plays. In such *covert* translations, no elements of the original are physically present in the

translation[9].

10. In most cases, a translated text will appear to its audience as a *manifest translation*, that is a text with a confirmed status as translation. Thus, if the identity of the author of a novel is communicated to the reader (see source text parameter 11), the identity of the translator will most often be revealed too. Typically, in translated books the translator will be credited on the title page – with his or her name set in smaller print than the author's, however – and most subtitled films and TV programs will credit their translators in a special subtitle. By contrast, genres like computer games and manuals for commercial products – often representing half a dozen languages in one booklet – will have neither the names of authors nor translators mentioned anywhere. Indeed, with such *concealed translations*, the notion of an original being translated may not always be useful. In such cases, rather than retaining the 'original vs. translation(s)' concept, one might talk about 'parallel texts', each serving the needs of specific markets that use different languages[10].

As opposed to the two cases outlined above, *pseudo-translations* are originals that fake their status as translations. In some cultures and genres, (literary) imports have higher prestige than domestic products, thus this inventive technique when, for example the subject matter or the setting is exotic enough to justify the invention of an original. This is sometimes seen in modern women's magazines, for instance in Denmark, where exotic and romantic short stories are published with English-sounding author pseudonyms, their (non-existing) translators not credited. However, there have been instances where authors have credited themselves as translators, for instance in the case of a "Nordic" novel presented to the German audience in (pseudo)translation about a century ago[11].

---

[9] For the terms 'overt' and 'covert' I am indebted to Juliane House (House 1981, 189 & 194) and K. Battarbee (1986).

[10] This kind of concealed translation is now often referred to with the buzzword *localization* – the term itself indicating the priority of pragmatic and commercial considerations over the quest for verbal equivalence between translations and originals.

[11] This example, as well as the term *pseudo-translation,* is taken from Gideon Toury

11. In most translational situations, two-way communication between translator and audience is not possible. This is true not only of all written translations, but of screen translation as well. To be precise, the term 'two-way communication' refers to immediate contact between the two parties involved; a letter to the publisher, for instance, complaining about a recently published translation, does not count. But for certain types of oral translation, verbal communication between audience and translator is indeed possible, even necessary. Thus, in community interpreting, the interplay between the parties involved is a *sine qua non*. Typically, we talk about three individuals here: an official, speaking only the majority language, an 'ethnic' client speaking a minority language, and the interpreter, often a native speaker of the minority language in question. Unlike almost all other translators, the community interpreter translates both ways within the confines of one 'text', i.e. one interpreting session. As a mediator, the interpreter is thus able to present questions to both parties concerning the interpretation – in a literal sense – of what was just said. The opposite is true of simultaneous interpreting. Here, the listening audience – typically conference participants – have no means of giving verbal feedback to the interpreter in the booth; a case of one-way communication.
12. The last transfer parameter, that of diversification, refers to the (im)possibility of supplying different language versions to different members of an audience. Such diversification is not normally found within a given society; the standard notion of 'one size fits all' is still a dogma with most text types. However, there are at least two exceptions: special – usually abridged – translations of novels and fairytales aimed at children (or adults with slight reading difficulties), and subtitles for domestic language minorities, e.g. the new Russian immigrants in Israel[12]. Technically, it is quite feasible to take diversifi-

---

(Toury 1995), who dedicates a whole chapter to this phenomenon.

[12] See Kaufmann 1998. In Israel, as in Finland and Belgium, most cinema subtitles are bilingual, with one subtitle row for Hebrew / Finnish / Dutch speakers, and the other row for those in the audience speaking Arabic / Swedish / French.

cation a step further, providing a range of minority groups with their 'personal' TV translations, via simultaneously transmitted teletext-generated subtitles. In this way, slow readers might select a heavily condensed version, readers with poor eyesight could have access to large-letter subtitles, language minorities could get subtitles in their native tongue, etc. With increased computerization of all media, including books, and with the good will of publishers, TV stations and other institutions involved, such optional translations ought to gain ground in years to come. Thus, the now-classical notion of 'equivalence of effect', recently expressed by Danish translator Thomas Harder[13], may one day come close to being realized.

Part II: SUBTITLING – THEORETICAL BACKGROUND

4.1 The fundamentals of subtitling

In the context of translation, and expressed in general and rather technical terms, subtitling consists in

> the rendering in a different language (1)
> of verbal messages (2)
> in filmic media (3),
> in the shape of one or more lines of written text (4),
> presented on the screen (5)
> in sync with the original verbal message (6).

ad 1) This basic sub-condition excludes intralingual subtitling, typically subtitling for the deaf and hard of hearing[14].

ad 2) These verbal messages include not only speech (film dialogue, commentary etc.) but also *displays* (written signs, e.g. newspaper headlines and street signs, "seen" by the camera), and *captions* (superimposed titles indicating for instance the profession of interviewees, added in post-production).

ad 3) Filmic media include cinema, video, television, laser disk and

---

[13] To Harder, the aim is to make sure that – as far as possible – translated text elements "carry the same potential for experience in the translation as in the original" ["så vidt muligt giver samme oplevelsesmuligheder i oversættelsen som i originalen"]. (Harder 1995, 17, my translation.)

[14] For a thorough discussion of this type of subtitling, see de Linde & Kay (1999).

DVD (digital versatile disk).

ad 4) Subtitle lines may be read left to right (e.g. with languages using Latin, Cyrillic or Greek alphabets) or right to left (e.g. with writing in Arabic or Hebrew).

ad 5) Subtitles need not be *'sub'*. In some countries, TV stations accept subtitles on the top of the screen in cases where important visual information is found in the lower fifth of the picture. Subtitles need not be horizontal, either. In Japan, vertical subtitles are some times used to supplement horizontal subtitling.

ad 6) Normally, subtitles are cued in advance, allowing for absolute synchrony. With news items, and on TV stations not yet equipped with state-of-the-art subtitling units, subtitles – though prepared in advance – are cued *on air*, in real time. Due to human physiology, this causes a delay of approximately one third of a second. Still, such subtitling must be considered synchronous, as opposed to simultaneous subtitling, in which not only cueing, but also the phrasing of subtitles is performed in real time, leading to massive delay.

4.2 Subtitling: a unique type of translation

As a basis for comparison with other main types of translation, subtitling can be defined – semiotically – as

A Prepared communication
B using written language
C acting as an additive
D and synchronous semiotic channel,
E as part of a transient
F and polysemiotic text.

In the table below, subtitling and four other central types of translation – dubbing, (performed) drama translation, literary translation and simultaneous interpreting – are juxtaposed, using the six features A through F as a basis for comparison:

In many ways a hybrid between classical forms of translation, subtitling shares the crucial feature B with literary translation – both operate in the written mode – and features E and F (real-time flow and semiotic complexity) with drama translation. All three types, plus dubbing, share feature A. As *artistic* types of language transfer, none of them are gen-

	Prepared	Written	Additive	Synchronous	Transient	Polysemiotic
Subtitling	+	+	+	+	+	+
Dubbing	+	–	–	+	+	+
Drama transl	+	–	–	–	+	+
Literary transl	+	+	–	–	–	–
Sim. interpret.	–	–	–	0	+	–

erated on the spot, in real life situations, as is simultaneous interpreting. The *pragmatic* nature of interpreting is also marked by the fact that style is largely irrelevant, something one could hardly say of any of the artistic types, including subtitling.

4.3 Diagonal subtitling: from foreign dialogue to domestic writing

Literary translation and interpreting, the two traditional counterparts in interlingual communication, are *horizontal* types, moving in a straight line from one human language to another, without shifting language mode: speech remains speech, and writing remains writing.

Subtitling, on the other hand, can be either *vertical* or *diagonal*. Being intralingual, vertical subtitling limits itself to taking speech down in writing, whereas diagonal subtitling, being interlingual, 'jaywalks' (crosses over) from source-language (SL) speech to target-language (TL) writing, as illustrated below:

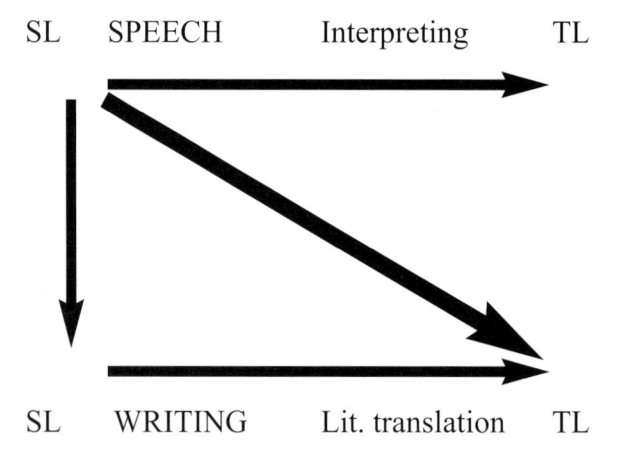

```
SL    SPEECH        Interpreting        TL




SL    WRITING       Lit. translation    TL
```

Due to its obliqueness, diagonal subtitling used to be considered an ugly duckling or even a non-translation. One of the pioneers of translation studies postulated:

"*Translation between media is impossible* (i.e. one cannot 'translate' from the *spoken* to the *written* form of a text or vice-versa)."
(Catford 1965, 53)

I quite agree that in the everyday sense of the word, you cannot translate from one medium to another. According to our initial definition, a novel, for instance, cannot be 'translated' into a movie. But by expanding the concept of translation, as Roman Jakobson, a contemporary of Catford, did (see Jakobson 1966), the term *intersemiotic translation* can be applied to the transfer between semiotically different entities – a case in point being screen adaptation, in which written stories are transformed into films.

However, subtitling – vertical or diagonal – is *intra*semiotic; it operates within the confines of the audiovisual media, and stays within the code of verbal language. The subtitler does not even alter the original; he or she adds an element, but does not delete any part of the audiovisual whole.

The problem, however, is that the graphemic subtitles should correspond with the phonemic dialogue that the subtitles should double. And the incompatibility of the oral and the written sub-codes alone can indeed act as a hindrance to the intended correspondence. In a handbook for British ('vertical') subtitlers, the dream of harmonious brotherhood between speech and writing is ruptured:

"The attempt to achieve perfect subtitling has some affinity to the search for the Holy Grail. The differing design features of written and spoken languages dictate that a perfect correspondence between the two cannot obtain." (Baker, Lambourne and Rowston 1984, 6)

If we settle for something slightly less than perfect, we would have to locate the differences between the two verbal sub-codes involved as well as their differing contexts.

The features distinguishing spoken from written communication are:
1) The interlocutors are in direct contact with each other; via their dialogue they share a situation. This produces an *implicit language* where

things can be taken for granted. Written sources usually need to explicate and extend the message, as the reader is unknown, or at least not present.
2) Spoken language has different *esthetic* norms, including a different categorization of certain stylistic features on the axes correct – incorrect, and formal – informal.

In addition, in *spontaneous speech* (genuine, as in talk shows, or acted, as in feature films) the subtitler will often find:
3) Pauses, false starts, self-corrections and interruptions.
4) Unfinished sentences and 'grammatically unacceptable' constructions.
5) Slips of the tongue, self-contradictions, ambiguities and nonsense.
6) Overlapping speech, a feature very difficult to render in writing.

Finally, it is characteristic of certain real or ficticious persons that:
7) Their language contains dialectal or sociolectal features that the established orthography is unable to cope with.
8) Their language contains idiolectal features, i.e. idiosyncrasies specific to the speaker.
9) Their pronunciation of certain words may be so indistinct that these words defy identification.

Thus, in diagonal subtitling, one must, on top of translating utterances from one language to another, transfer the dialogue from one sub-code (the seemingly unruly spoken language) to another (the more rigid written language). If this shift of sub-code was not performed as a fundamental part of the subtitling process, the audience would be taken aback by reading the oddities of spoken discourse. But as the dialogue is always re-coded on the way to the bottom of the screen, people only react if the other dimension of diagonal subtitling – the translation proper – seems imperfect.

However, evaluating subtitles as translation is not easy either. Because of the complex, polysemiotic nature of film and TV, a comparison between subtitles and (transcribed) dialogue will not suffice for making adequacy judgments. In the case of book translations, a simple verbal text comparison will work, if factors such as difference in time, place and readership are considered. But when dealing with subtitling, the synthesis of four synchronous semiotic channels (image, sound, dialogue and subtitles) should be compared with the original three-channel discourse. Severed from the audiovisual context, neither subtitles nor dialogue will render the full meaning of the film. So in judging the quality of subtitles, one must examine the degree to which the subtitled version *as a whole* manages to convey the semantic gestalt of the original.

4.4 Subtitling speech acts: words in the balance

Every translational act forces the translator to make priorities. Different media and different types of discourse naturally impose different constraints, or – to put it more optimistically – leave the translator with different sets of clues for dealing with the particular issues at stake. Thus, subtitling does not differ from literary translation in that it constrains the translator, but rather because the constraints of an audiovisual context are different from those of the patient, yet impotent paper[15].

In rendering what human voices are trying to express, be that in literature, films or TV fiction, there are no absolutes, no canonized solutions. But this fact should not be taken as an easy excuse for claiming that any phrasing is as good as the next. In subtitling, as in all types of translation, no word should be accidental, and even good ideas should be tested against alternative solutions. There is always more than one answer to a (subtitling) question, but even more 'solutions' that miss the target. And in order to hit that target, all relevant linguistic, esthetical and technical means should be utilized, and both dialogue, film and viewers must be considered.

In subtitling, the speech act is in focus; verbal intentions and visual effects are more important than lexical elements in isolation. This gives the subtitler a certain amount of linguistic freedom[16]. But the adequate rendering must seem self-evident to the viewers: the audience is not served with memorials of the plight of the subtitler. Only the results

---

[15] The formal and textual constraints of subtitling are discussed in Gottlieb 1997, 72-74.
[16] When dealing with non-fiction material, in which terminology plays a greater role, the freedom is markedly reduced: some TV documentaries, for instance, are so information dense that finding adequate expressions in the target language is no longer the question; the problem is rather fitting these often lenghtly and hard-to-read terms into the subtitles.

count, not the hours spent translating a sequence that some might classify as 'untranslatable'.

As stated earlier, subtitling is an *overt* type of translation which, by retaining the original version, lays itself bare to criticism from everybody with the slightest knowledge of the source language. At the same time, subtitles are *fragmentary* in that they only represent the lexical and the syntactic features of the dialogue. The prosodic features are not truly represented in subtitles: added exclamation marks, italics, etc. are only faint echoes of the certain ring that intonation gives the wording of the dialogue. Furthermore, subtitling has to manage without well-known literary and dramatic devices such as stage direction, author's remarks, footnotes, etc. The audience will have to turn to the original acoustic and visual clues in trying to grasp the meaning behind the words of the subtitles. And even with languages as different as Greek and Danish, monolinguals in both Denmark and Greece are able to pick up some of these extra-linguistic clues in the lines spoken in the opposite language.

4.5 Subtitle editing and the question of reduction

As the reader may have noticed, reduction in verbal content and form was not included among the defining features of subtitling discussed earlier in this paper (see sections 4.1 and 4.2). The reason for this is that most of the dialogue reduction represented in subtitles follows directly from the diasemiotic nature of subtitling. In other words, the deletion or condensation of redundant, oral features is a necessity when crossing over from speech to writing.

Still, subtitles are often condensed beyond this point. This may be a result of esthetic considerations – as when a subtitler wants to minimize the number of lines covering the action on the screen – or motivated by reading speed concerns[17]. Especially with up-tempo speech, the subtitler may choose to sacrifice close to 50% of the dialogue – measured in quantita-

---

[17] In Britain, "the average reading speed of adult viewers is estimated at 66% of the average speaking speed", according to the Independent Television Commission (de Linde & Kay 1999, 11). This happens to coincide with the fact that in Europe, most subtitlers semi-intuitively reduce the dialogue by around one third, most of this reduction caused by the economy of the written code in comparison with speech.

tive terms – in order not to exceed the normal television 'speed limit'. This limit, of some twelve subtitle characters per second (12 cps), means that a full two-liner should stay on the screen for at least five seconds. Before rushing out to declare subtitling a reductive translation mode after all, it is worth noting that the 12 cps limit is based on the assumption that 90% of the viewers should be able to follow the subtitles. Acknowledging young people's increasing sensitivity to written messages onscreen, and knowing that already a generation ago around 50% of the viewers read a two-liner within three seconds, (Hanson 1974) it takes little effort to conclude that if subtitling speeds should reflect the present reading capacity of most viewers, no 'harmful' cuts were needed in subtitling for the general audience. Still, slow-reading poorly educated people without many foreign language skills still comprise a significant minority of the viewers in subtitling countries, and these heavy and loyal users of television should not be alienated by fast and complex subtitles. However, with digital TV just around the corner, an array of different subtitle versions could be transmitted simultaneously. In this way, slow and laidback viewers could select a subtitle option pretty much like the one they are used to, while fast and curious readers could go for a more complete version, with hardly any loss of semantic and stylistic information in the subtitles. In part III of this paper, I will elaborate on this scenario.

Closing the discussion on reduction in subtitling, I will point to the fact that due to intersemiotic redundancy (positive feedback from visuals and soundtrack) much current reduction in subtitling is neutralized, so viewers miss less of the content of the film than a merely linguistic analysis might indicate. Put differently: in a polysemiotic context, semantic voids are often intersemiotically filled. Subtitle reading can be compared to a cloze test, in which "le spectateur (...) accepte de reconstruire mentalement ces parties des conversations qui manquent, mais dont la présence est virtuelle." (Tomaszkiewicz 1993, 267)

Sometimes seen as the epitome of subtitling, the tendency to condense speech is also found in other types of translation, e.g. consecutive interpreting and voice-over. Among the oral traits thus prone to condensation are colloquialisms, slang, cursing, pragmatic particles and repetitions. It is obvious that the trimming of the discourse through the elimination of such features in translation not only leads to quantitative reductions; it is also instrumental in *normalizing* the text, by presenting the target-language audience with a version less non-standard than the original. This in turn explains why subtitling is not the only form of translation displaying condensation of the original dialogue. The time-and-space constraints of subtitling are often just an easy excuse for leaving out 'controversial' elements of the original dialogue.

4.6 Stylistic normalization: centripetal forces at work

Many subtitled films and TV programs show clear signs of normalization, which implies the replacement of non-standard verbal elements by standard ones, typically resulting in reduced text volume. As has been proved by Olivier Goris (Goris 1993), such normalization is also commonly found in dubbing, a type of translation seldom in need of condensed solutions.

An interesting element in this global strategy of standardization is the commonly used local strategy of explicitation, often found even in subtitling – another reason for not considering condensation a defining factor in subtitling. By expliciting 'obscure' points in the original – sometimes beyond recognition – the translator may serve his audience well, but this strategy may imply sheer banalization of the text, which may in the end lose the very qualities that fascinated the source-language audience, and justified its translation in the first place.

Through the strategy of normalization, including explicitation, the translator moves the text away from its original and, literally speaking, often excentric position within its genre, pulling it into a position which is less extreme. In this way, both at a general level (the entire text) and at a more specific one (e.g. the individual sentence) 'excentric' originals are often sucked inward, toward the center of the genre in question. This phenomenon, which we will diagnose as the *centripetal effect in translation*, is best illustrated this way, the 'X' in the figures representing the text in question:

Original position in the genre: New position in the genre:

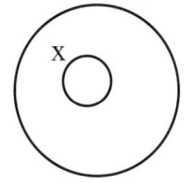

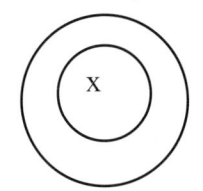

As a result of this 'law of culture', translated – and thus subtitled – products often come out as less emotional, less ambiguous and less bizarre than their original counterparts. This means that what we read in the subtitles is often less personal, less insulting or less funny than what the source-language actors said and meant.

In defense of the mainstreaming of many audiovisual products one may argue that without such normalization, the original film or TV series might have dropped outside the circle of acceptance in the target culture. And more often than not, mainstreaming may be better than condemnation. In the final analysis, however, subtitling *per se* is not to blaim for watered-out dialogue; the target-culture norms and the individual subtitler will have to share the honor of normalization.

4.7 The different subtexts of subtitling

To Danes and Greeks alike, subtitling is an integral part of their culture. This is due to the fact that in all "former" Western European speech communities with less than 25 million speakers, foreign-language films and TV programs are subtitled rather than dubbed.

In subtitling countries, reading subtitles while watching the action on the screen has become second nature to the literate population, i.e. some 92 percent of all adults and older children (Elbro 1989). Here, neither lip-sync dubbing (Herbst 1995) nor voice-over – a non-synchronous technique common in Russia, Poland and the Baltic countries (Dries 1994-95; Grigaraviciute & Gottlieb 1999) – are acceptable to viewers; revoicing of the original soundtrack is only found in material aimed at very young audiences[18].

In some subtitling countries, even children's films come in subtitled versions. According to Greek subtitler Iannis Papadakis, "the subtitling

---

[18] In recent years, however, both Greece and Denmark have witnessed the introduction of lip-sync dubbing on TV and video productions for general audiences. In Greece, certain soap operas are now dubbed on commercial TV (personal communication with Greek subtitling researcher Stavroula Sokoli, October 1999). In Denmark, beginning in 1996 with *Free Willy II*, dubbed versions of such family feature films as *Lassie, The Borrowers, Flubber* and *Dr. Dolittle* have been introduced on the video market, often in a "two for the price of one" deal, with both versions (the dubbed and the subtitled film) on the same VHS tape. (Gottlieb (forthcoming)).

tradition is so strong in Greece that Disney regularly releases excellent dubbed versions of animated films like "Lion King" and "Pocahontas" for young audiences, *and subtitled versions for the adult audience.*" (Papadakis 1998, 70, emphasis added.)

In dubbing countries – i.e. Spain, Italy and the German- and French-speaking parts of Europe – there is nothing "childish" about dubbing. In those countries, subtitling foreign-language films is the odd solution, reserved for special audiences, e.g. Woody Allen aficionados or Monty Python buffs. As foreign languages are hardly ever heard on TV or cinema screens in such (major) speech communities, subtitling is often seen as something alien, even by scholars in the field. In France, for instance, the term 'subtitling' – or rather 'sous-titrage' – has a set of connotations at odds with those found in countries where subtitling is a household word:

> Puisque le sous-titrage en France a servi depuis plus de 60 ans de seul critère objectif dans la classification de film "d'art" [...], le sous-titrage a fini par devenir label de qualité et signifier "cinéma d'art" même dans le cas de films que la plupart des cinéphiles ne jugeraient pas a priori particulièrement "artistiques".
> (Danan 1995, 277)

The semi-conscious linking of 'art movies' and subtitles mentioned by Danan are not found in countries where subtitling is the prevalent form of screen translation and where most cinema films and television series are imported.

In Britain and the United States, the two leading film and TV exporters, even the notion of 'foreign' films or TV programs, no matter how these are presented to the domestic audience, has an exotic ring to large segments of the population. Today, subtitled films may be even less attractive than a decade or two ago:

> [...] subtitles are the sticking point for English-speaking audiences. The more literary style of foreign film is demanding enough, but it is made all the more challenging by the need to read along with the performance. The generation that Hollywood blockbusters are deliberately catering for, the 16- to 24-year-olds, is one that, in one distributor's words, is "growing increasingly lazy and unlikely ever to

go back to subtitling". (Finney 1997, 8)

And in pro-dubbing Germany, even an *Anglizist* (with a profound knowledge of the linguistic pitfalls of dubbing) considers subtitling something outlandish; attractive at first glance, perhaps, but a practice that may lead unsuspecting viewers astray:

> There can hardly be any doubt that, from a foreign language teaching perspective, subtitling is much to be preferred to dubbing [...], but it is equally clear that as far as translational equivalence is concerned, subtitling has obvious disadvantages. In particular *one must be very sceptical of any suggestion that listening to the original text in a language you do not speak yourself still enables you to get some idea of a character's personality* because you are, after all, listening to the original voices. Precisely because there are some important differences between what you might call the paralinguistic systems of different languages as well, the viewer might arrive at totally wrong conclusions. (Herbst 1995, 258; emphasis added)

The arguments above are irrefutable per se, but they rest on the faulty assumption that the audience not only do not understand the language spoken on screen; they do not even know how to decode paraverbal elements in the dialogue, typically intonation patterns.

However, viewers in subtitling countries do indeed understand the paraverbal features in most of the languages they are ever going to hear on TV; they even manage to understand important parts of the dialogue in most subtitled films and TV episodes, since between sixty and ninety percent of all imported productions in subtitling countries are Anglophone – roughly the same percentage as that of English speakers in several of those countries.

Ironically, part of the reason that for instance most Scandinavians are now well-versed in English is the national preference for subtitling in their countries: keine Hexerei, nur Behändigkeit!

Part III: SUBTITLING IN DENMARK

5.1 Subtitles – the only genre read by all

In Denmark – as in the rest of Scandinavia – subtitling has established itself as one of the dominant written text types in public life: by 1993 the average Dane spent more than three and a half hours (217 minutes) a week reading TV and video subtitles – en effort equating four English lessons each week. The reading of printed translations only accounted for a little less than two hours a week[19]. With TV and video consumption still on the increase, and with the heavy reliance of new, commercial TV channels on foreign (= American) imports, most Danes are likely to read even more interlingual subtitles in the years to come. Several segments of the population are now shifting from reading newspapers (youth and women) and books (middle-aged men) to relying mainly on TV and the Internet for new information and entertainment. To many Danes, the subtitles on TV is what keeps their reading abilities alive; an unintended, yet important, side effect of the choice of translation practice in Denmark.

5.2 "It's all Greek to me"– when subtitlers fail to understand

In Scandinavia, one rarely encounters film or TV dialogue in Greek, and when it does happen, it may surprise even the subtitler. An example of this was demonstrated some years ago by Sveriges Television, Sweden's public-service broadcasting corporation. In an episode of the renowned detective series *Inspector Morse,* set in Oxford – carrying the classical title *Greeks Bearing Gifts* – and broadcast in January 1993, a verbal exchange in Greek was left untranslated. Although the scene in question was of importance to the plot, the Swedish translator, apparently knowing no Greek, only managed to come up with one subtitle: a trans-

---

[19] The figures are based on earlier studies, showing that during 22 per cent of the time spent watching TV, Danes were presented with (interlingual) subtitles on the screen (see Gottlieb 1994, 149). According to the official *Danish Cultural and Media Statistics 1980-1992* (106; 128), in 1992 the private TV consumption amounted to 17 hours and 16 minutes a week per Dane (above the age of 13). Adding to this, members of video households (46% of all homes, now almost 90%) watched video 3 hours a week. (Source: the Danmarks Radio weekly, *DRåben,* no. 6, 1993.)

lation of some totally irrelevant lines uttered by the actors in a soap opera that one of the Greeks was watching on TV. The reason: those lines were in English, a language understood by all subtitlers in Scandinavia – and by most of their viewers[20].

Another product of the sad, but common lack of source-language knowledge in subtitlers working with films from minor speech communities – in casu Greece – is found in the 'official' Danish video version of Theodoros Angelopoulos' *O Melissokomos* (the Beekeeper), in Danish *Biavleren*, distributed by the national Statens Filmcentral. In this film from 1987, featuring the Italian (!) actor Marcello Mastroianni, most of the dialogue is in Greek, with French spoken in one of the scenes. Still, what the Danish audience gets, is English-sounding Danish subtitles, indicating that this film has not been translated from Greek (and French), but from English – a case of pivot translation, with all the problems this implies (see section 5.4). Adding to this, the subtitler of *O Melissokomos*, apparently working from a script instead of a videotape, produced oddities such as using wrong gender (*det* instead of *den*) of objects clearly visible on the screen – a type of error bound to happen in careless translation from a language lacking the grammatical distinctions of the target language. In not checking their subtitles against the image, script-addicted subtitlers are prone to committing such mistakes, even if they know the source language(s) of the films they work with.

5.3 Silent movies, speaking titles

Although not as established as literary translation, which has existed for millenia, subtitling is certainly coming of age. Based on an ancient tradition of supplementing pictures with captioned text, the procedure of captioning film dialogue has now been around for almost a hundred years.

It all began with the *intertitles* of the silent movies. They first ap-

---

[20] Recent figures show that more than 80% of the adolescent and adult Danish population speak English (Davidsen-Nielsen 1998, 87). This does not mean, however, that a majority would be able to understand the English dialogue presented on Danish TV screens in the way native speakers do.

peared in Edward S. Porter's *Uncle Tom's Cabin* from 1903[21]. In Denmark, which in the infancy of motion pictures held a strong position as a film nation, intertitles appeared on the scene in 1907[22]. These titles were photographed cardboard signs with printed text – often using beautifully elaborated letters – that were cut into the film itself, thus filling the entire screen. *Line titles,* the equivalent of sound film subtitles, were not found in the first silent movies. Instead, *epic titles* were used.

The Danish silent film expert, Marguerite Engberg, distinguishes between three types of epic titles: the commenting, the anticipating, and those simply indicating time or place. Epic intertitles could be used as a means of making a (sometimes awkward) cinematic description understandable to the audience. The director might comment on the action with the title "A difficult task well done", or anticipate the course of events with "Armand immediately falls in love". In case time or place could not be indicated with purely filmic effects, one had to resort to titles such as "One month later".

Already in 1909, the first line titles appeared in Danish movies. Throughout the years, until the appearance of the sound film in the late 1920s, line titles made up an increasing part of the intertitles. This was due to the filmmakers' greater mastery of the medium: many of the epic titles could be expressed through merely filmic devices, but the actors' lines often had to be rendered in words. Still, a good silent film of the usual c. 45 minutes could work splendidly with about 20 titles – some 5% of the amount one would expect in a modern (sound) movie of the same duration.

Outside of Denmark, directors such as Griffith and Eisenstein made films with far more intertitles; *October,* for one, had 270. But no matter the number and type of intertitles in a foreign film; they had to be translated. This was done by cutting out the original intertitles and replacing them with similar titles in the domestic language, often with the effect that imported films took an extra liking to snapping during projection.

It should be pointed out that even in the days of the silent film, writing was often found in the picture: Apart from inserts of letters, telegrams,

---

[21] According to Marleau 1982, 272.
[22] The source of this and much of the following information is Engberg 1977 (171-173).

names on doors, etc. – so-called displays – there were, in some cases, superimposed captions on the screen. For example, in a sequence of the French film *Judex* from 1917, a caption is placed on a wall, between two people. This is recorded in Guinness' *Movie Facts and Feats* as the oldest (French) example of movie subtitles[23].

Perhaps the oldest example of an entire film being captioned, or subtitled, is the silent movie *Mireille* from 1922. In this film the titles were placed at the bottom of the screen, below the picture – which for this occasion was reduced – so they could be watched simultaneously with the film.

This very *synchrony* makes the crucial difference between the old intertitles and the new subtitles, which with the coming of sound ousted the well-known cardboard signs from the world of film.

5.4 The subtitling of sound films

The world's first sound movie, *The Jazz Singer* from late 1927 – starring Al Jolson – was shown in non-English-speaking countries with subtitles, though not until a few years later. The sequel to this film, *The Singing Fool*, also featuring Al Jolson and released in the US in 1928, reached Denmark before its predecessor.

Its first showing in Denmark was on August 17, 1929. The film was titled *Den Syngende Nar* and fitted with Danish subtitles. The following morning, in the major Danish daily, *Berlingske Tidende*, a journalist wrote:

> It is most annoying to have unsatisfactory Danish subtitles presented in the picture while the characters speak their lines in English [...] but, of course, we are only at the beginning.
> (Translated from Dinnesen & Kau 1983, 44)

In France, *The Jazz Singer* had had its first showing in Paris, on January 26, 1929, with subtitles in French. After the initial enthusiasm concerning this and other early (subtitled) sound films, the French audience grew increasingly dissatisfied with the whole idea of subtitling (cf. Danan 1996, 114). France soon turned to dubbing, as did other major European countries, notably Italy, which had also had a flirt with subtitling in 1929

---

[23] The information on French intertitles is mostly based on Brant 1984.

(cf. Quargnolo 1986). Holland started subtitling in 1930 – and remained faithful to this method – and in January 1932, subtitling made its debut in Great Britain (cf. Bruls & Kerkman 1988). By 1933, the method of subtitling had established itself internationally.

However, this breakthrough was not due to a wish to retain the original soundtrack so audiences abroad could enjoy the voices of the original actors. Neither was it due to a cosmopolitan view that it would be beneficial for people to hear foreign tongues. Whatever attitudes on language policy expressed later on in minor speech communities that are now opposed to dubbing, these countries originally favored subtitling due to economic necessity. Dubbing was simply not feasible.

In their monumental work, *Filmen i Danmark,* film historians Dinnesen and Kau state this fact without further ado: "The process was difficult, cumbersome, and far too expensive to be worthwhile in a small country like Denmark." (Translated from Dinnesen & Kau, 54).

In Denmark, as in many other countries, people had to live with subtitled movies – and they still do.

5.5 Subtitling on television

The TV medium followed closely in the footsteps of the film. On August 14, 1938 – a year before the outbreak of World War II – the BBC broadcast the German silent film *Der Student von Prag* (1913), with the inserted English cinema titles. According to a veteran BBC subtitler, it was "perhaps the first scheduled public transmission of a feature film in high-definition television history." (Minchinton1987, 282). Thus, even television started with intertitles, and only in countries that already subtitled sound films did TV broadcasting companies opt for subtitling in this new mass medium. In major speech communities, dubbing was preferred on TV as on the silver screen.

In Denmark, Julius Bomholt, then Chairman of the Radio Council, declared Danish television "on the air" on October 2, 1951, though for the first three years Danmarks Radio (DR) only broadcast 3 hours a week. All productions were broadcast live from a studio, and in the beginning, they were all in Danish.

Before introducing subtitling in 1955, DR had its first foreign-language productions translated by a film professor who read all the lines off-screen to the small, but enthusiastic Danish audience. However, this practice was canceled after the (male) professor had done his best to render three French girls in an agitated exchange of words (Skaarup 1981). Then the director general of DR interfered, and since that day no feature films have been voiced-over on Danish TV.

Not only was the choice of translation method a challenge; the purchase of foreign films proved to be all but impossible, as the film industry did its best to prevent DR from broadcasting cinema productions. Thus, the foreign programs consisted of documentaries and short entertainment films[24]. These films – most of them only 30 minutes long – were the first programs to be subtitled on Danish television, as early as 1955.

In the long run, however, it turned out to be impossible for Danish cinema owners to keep feature films from reaching the magic TV screens. In 1956, DR began to purchase film rights from abroad, and the year after, the Danish film establishment lamented:

> October 3. was a day of sorrow for most Danish cinema owners. The national television had obtained Hitchcock's famous film *Foreign Correspondent,* with famous stars in the leading roles, the result being that most of those who had the option preferred going to the free cinema at home, while the real cinemas were empty.
>
> (Translated from *Biografbladet*, no. 11, 1957, 256)

It goes without saying that Danish film importers did not want to rub salt into their own wounds by offering DR their Danish subtitles for these foreign movies.

5.5.1 Danish TV subtitling: the first generation

The early years

DR had no other option but to establish its own subtitling procedures right from the beginning. Programs were purchased without subtitles. The steadily increasing staff of freelance subtitlers thus provided the translation, layout, and (later on) application of the Danish subtitles. Between 1955 and 1957-58, translators' subtitles were written onto cardboard cards (not unlike the cardboard signs of silent movies), which were then photographed onto a subtitle film strip, from which each subtitle could

---

[24] For this and much of the following information, I am indebted to Peter Hansen, former technical manager of DR.

then be broadcast when it was cued.

This somewhat laborious procedure was replaced by a technique in which the subtitles were written onto subtitle signs photographed during transmission. These signs were then placed on three music stands, distributed like a deck of cards (e.g. no. 4 was underneath no. 1, etc.). By alternating between three cameras, the subtitles could be exposed in the correct order[25]. The subtitler directed three assistants, who had to turn the used subtitles over manually and thus bring the new ones into focus. DR only used this slightly farcical method for about a year.

The technique in the '60s end '70s

In the winter of 1958-59 DR launched a new technique. During broadcasting, the Danish subtitles, typewritten on a paper roll, were projected onto the film picture. The subtitler had to advance the roll, subtitle by subtitle, and press a button that activated a camera that photographed the subtitle. This optical method – in those days called *electronic subtitling* – was used by DR right up till 1981-82, i.e. for 23 years. When it first appeared, the method was advanced, as even into the 1960s, several European broadcasting services were still using large index cards or signs for TV subtitling.

In those days, a number of countries broadcast the original cinema version with etched or superimposed subtitles. DR did this as well on a few occasions, giving rise to the well-known contrast problem: subtitles 'disappearing' against a bright background. This was also a problem for the 'electronic' TV subtitling produced at Danmarks Radio. To solve this, a black bar was inserted at the bottom of the picture during transmission. This so-called 'liquorice band' is completely transparent on a dark background, but the brighter the picture, the blacker the band appears. In this way, the necessary contrast to the white subtitle characters is provided.

For many years, Danish TV subtitles were centered, just as cinema subtitles were, and still are. But in the 1970s they became left-aligned, for cost-saving reasons! The fact was that in those pre-wordprocessing days

---

[25] A vivid description of this kind of subtitling and its problems is found in Skaarup 1981.

it took the typists too long to center all the subtitles, line by line, on their electric IBM typewriters. The makeshift solution of left alignment has since become the norm, also for modern Danish electronic TV and video subtitling, even though the subtitler may now center all subtitles in a TV program within a matter of seconds.

In the early '60s DR had tried to feed subtitles automatically, but the method was soon abandoned. The technique was as follows: the subtitler had to mark those places on an audiotape where subtitles should appear and disappear. During transmission, the subtitle paper roll would automatically advance to the proper subtitles at the right moments, so that the camera could project them onto the film. The system was vulnerable, however, and if errors occurred it was impossible to return to the place where the subtitles failed. The film had to be rewound and played from the top, which wasn't too popular with the viewers.

5.5.2 Danish TV subtitling: the second generation

From paper manuscript to disk

In the summer of 1981, DR returned to automatic feeding, this time for good. Denmark was one of the first countries in the world to switch to actual electronic subtitling. For this method, the subtitler still wrote his or her subtitles on paper. Manuscript typists then transferred them manually to an 8-inch floppy disk. On this disk the subtitler would set the in- and out-cues of each subtitle, while playing back a time-coded U-matic videotape of the program. When the program was broadcast, the film signal – from a 2-inch broadcasting tape with time code – would automatically connect with the subtitles.

Now the subtitler could take time off during transmission, and the subtitling could have the technical, esthetic, and linguistic quality that he or she was able to give it. The system was reliable, though sometimes a technician might insert the wrong disk into the drive. The technique wasn't foolproof.

All-electronic subtitling

In 1988-89, Danmarks Radio introduced a new and fully electronic form of subtitling, as did several other European TV stations. With this method, all intermediate stages were skipped. The subtitles were fed in the same way as described above, but the writing, editing and cueing was now done in one procedure – on small, PC-based subtitling units, many of which were still in use ten years later.

In October 1988, Danish TV2 launched a wave of new Danish channels to hit the national TV screens. Still in 2000, most of the subtitles broadcast by these stations and usually produced by subcontractors, conform to the norms of DR, technically as well as in terms of phrasing and design (cf. Lindberg/Søndergaard 1997). As far as translational quality is concerned, some stations fare better than others. While the three public-service channels (DR1, DR2 and TV2) keep a decent standard, various satellite channels display a somewhat poorer quality. However, the worst subtitles in Denmark today seem to be those broadcast (terrestrially) by the fourth Danish station, TV-Danmark. A collection of recent translation blunders from this station can be accessed on special Internet sites[26].

Today, most of the Danish subtitling industry uses Windows-based subtitling software, with sophisticated cueing facilities, spellcheckers, etc. in a multitasking environment. This means that subtitlers have simultaneous access to electronic dictionaries and Internet websites while using the workstations's own features. The technical developments in subtitling may thus be impressive, but in the last analysis, the working conditions in the business and the personal integrity and talent in the subtitlers is what count. The Danish stations criticized the most for their subtitles are not stuck with outdated technology – they just don't realize that quality subtitles is a must in the competetive world of modern television.

---

[26] Not included in TitleVision's normal list of howlers (*Bøfsiden*), lists of blunders broadcast by TV-Danmark can be found on the sites www.titlevision.dk/tvd-kboeuf.htm and www.jeronimus.subnet.dk (as of January 2000).

5.6 The future: Pivot translation or personal subtitles?

A new potential source of errors in the world of electronic subtitling is found in the increasing use of pivot translations (as described in section 3.1). Satellite transmissions across language barriers make pivot subtitling a financially attractive method of subtitling major-language material for a series of smaller speech communities, often simultaneously broadcast – via satellite.

As with any pivot translation, pivot subtitling is used where the pivot language is closer to – or more well-known in – the target language (culture) than the source language is. But in the process of subtitling, where the translation proper only accounts for a part of the work and money invested, a prospective pivot language need not be particularly close to the target language in question: as long as the segmentation and cueing can be 'borrowed' from the pivot subtitles, time and money are saved. However, the practice of pivot subtitling implies four potential pitfalls which are not normally found in subtitling:

1) Repetition of translation errors present in the pivot subtitles;
2) Transfer of pivot-language features not acceptable in the target language;
3) Transfer of segmentation incompatible with target language syntax;
4) Transfer of subtitle layout and cueing inferior to existing national standards[27].

Pivot subtitling is also found in the home video market, but rather than staying a somewhat grotesque exception to normal practices, it is gaining ground: already in 1993, TV3, the largest TV channel in Scandinavia, transmitting all programs from London via satellite, utilized this method in no less than 80% of its Danish programing, and by 1999, the pivot technique had spread to all non-public service TV channels in Denmark. The standard procedure is as follows: in Copenhagen the Dan-

---

[27] To be fair, well-made pivot versions may clear the ground of semantic land mines, thus yielding better target-language results than might otherwise have been achieved, presuming that the target-language subtitlers are lesser talents. But without this presumption, pivot subtitling is not to be trusted as a safety net in the circus of screen translation.

ish subtitler receives the (master) subtitle file in disk format or via email, and then it is up to him or her to produce a Danish version. As the subtitler is not paid to do any cueing, the original – typically, Swedish – rhythm of segmentation, often different from Danish practice, is followed (cf. type 4 above). This means fewer subtitles per minute, and consequently, heavier dialogue reduction than in normal subtitling into Danish.

The fact that the four above-mentioned types of errors are often documented on Danish TV screens (cf. note 26) turns modern teletext and subtitling technology into a mixed blessing. But just as it gives owners of satellite-based commercial TV stations the opportunity to buy clusters of (poorly) subtitled versions at bargain prices, modern technology opens up an alternative scenario: *personal subtitling*. By using this term I refer to a situation in which, for the first time, the viewer is able to choose, not just between different target languages, but between different styles or levels of subtitling, by selecting different teletext pages on his remote control unit. With sets of optional subtitles broadcast simultaneously, viewers watching a foreign-language program could choose, for instance, 1) a no-subtitling option, 2) fast, uncondensed subtitles, 3) normal-speed subtitles, 4) special subtitles for slow readers, 5) pictogram-supported subtitles for the deaf and hard of hearing, 6) subtitles in a domestic minority language, or finally, 7) foreign-learner subtitles in the source language[28].

Depending on the individual program and its expected target audience, different clusters of options could be offered, should TV companies consider five or six subtitle versions per program too costly. But as dubbing is 15 times as expensive as subtitling[29], even the full range of versions could be offered for just over one third of the language trans-

---

[28] The potential of teletext for viewer-specific subtitling was already explored nearly a decade ago (Jørgensen 1992).

[29] In 1991, the average cost of dubbing a one-hour TV program was 11,000 ECU, as opposed to 740 ECU for subtitling the same program (Luyken et al. 1991, 105). Due to fierce competition in the subtitling industry, prices for subtitling services have remained low throughout the 1990s. Thus, today's gap between the costs of the two methods may have widened even further.

fer price paid today in Europe's dubbing countries. Apart from sheer conservatism, the only obstacle to changing the present situation (with major speech communities dubbing all foreign-language programs and minor countries using 'one-size-fits-all' subtitles) is the fact that a substantial number of the existing TV sets lack the teletext facilities necessary for receiving optional subtitles. But this is just a matter of time; all TV sets sold in (Western) Europe nowadays come with teletext.

Already today, films on DVD (Digital Versatile Disk) are marketed in multi-language versions, with several optional dubbing tracks and subtitle files. Technically, it is possible to include as many as 8 dubbed and 32 subtitled versions on one disk, but most DVD films are marketed with "only" English, French and Spanish soundtracks and subtitles, i.e. six optional versions. With Digital Video Broadcasting (DVB) being introduced in the near future, new standards for TV translation will be set, making personal subtitling a matter of course to most audiences worldwide[30].

---

[30] For further details on the technological state of the art within screen translation, see Karamitroglou 1999.

References

Baker, Robert G.; Andrew D. Lambourne & Guy Rowston. 1984
Handbook for Television Subtitlers. IBA Engineering Division

Battarbee, K. 1986
Subtitles and soundtrack, in: *Trans,* 144-164.
School of Translation Studies, University of Turku

Brant, Rosemary. 1984
The History and Practice of French Subtitling
Unpublished MA thesis, University of Texas at Austin

Bruls, Emile & Ed Kerkman. 1988
Ondertiteling in Beeld. Unpublished MA thesis, University of Amsterdam

Catford, J.C. 1965
A Linguistic Theory of Translation. Oxford University Press, London

Danan, Martine. 1995
Le sous-titrage. Stratégie culturelle et commerciale
In: Gambier (ed.) 1995, 271-281

Davidsen-Nielsen, Niels. 1998.
Fordanskning af engelske låneord – Kan det nytte?
In: Erik Hansen & Jørn Lund (eds.) *Det er korrekt: Dansk retskrivning 1948-1998,* 79-93
Hans Reitzels Forlag, Copenhagen

De Linde, Zoé & Neil Kay. 1999
The Semiotics of Subtitling. St. Jerome Publishing, Manchester

Dinnesen, Niels Jørgen & Edvin Kau. 1983
Filmen i Danmark. Akademisk Forlag, Copenhagen

Dries, Josephine. 1994-95
Breaking Language Barriers behind the Broken Wall (voice-over, dubbing or subtitling?)
In: *Intermedia* vol. 22, no. 6, 35-37

Elbro, Carsten. 1989
Svage læsere og teksters tilgængelighed

In: *Nordisk tv-teksting,* 64-70. Nordisk Språksekretariat, Oslo

Engberg, Marguerite. 1977
Dansk stumfilm – de store år. Rhodos, København

Finney, Angus. 1997
Money talks, and it speaks English
In: *The Sunday Times,* Feb. 2, 1997, section 11, 8-9. London

Flintholm, Line. 1998
Én roman, to oversættelser: "Pascual Duarte" på dansk
(Danske Afhandlinger om Oversættelse 7), Center for Oversættelse, Engelsk Institut, University of Copenhagen

Gambier, Yves (ed.) 1995
Communication audiovisuelle et transferts linguistiques. Audiovisual communication and Language Transfer. Special issue of *Nouvelles de la FIT – FIT Newsletter,* vol. 14, nos. 3-4

Goris, Olivier. 1993
The question of French dubbing: Towards a frame for systematic investigation
In: *Target* vol. 5, no. 2, 169-190

Gottlieb, Henrik. 1994 (second printing 1998)
Tekstning – synkron billedmedieoversættelse
(Danske Afhandlinger om Oversættelse 5)
Center for Oversættelse, Engelsk Institut, University of Copenhagen

Gottlieb, Henrik. 1997
Subtitles, Translation & Idioms.
Center for Translation Studies, English Department, University of Copenhagen

Gottlieb, Henrik (forthcoming)
In Video Veritas: Are Danish voices less American than Danish subtitles?
In: Rosa Agust Canós & Frederic Chaume Varela (eds.) *Translation in the XXI Century.* (Estudis sobre la traducció 6), Universitat Jaume I Press, Castelló, Spain

Grigaraviciute, Ieva & Henrik Gottlieb. 1999
Danish voices, Lithuanian voice-over: The mechanics of non-synchro-

nous translation
In: *Perspectives: Studies in Translatology* 1: 1999, 41-80

Hanson, Göte. 1974.
Läsning av text i tv. SR/PUB 102/72. Sveriges Radio, Stockholm

Harder, Thomas. 1995
Litterær oversættelse i praksis
In: Peter Florentsen (ed.) *Oversættelse af litteratur,* 7-28
(Danske Afhandlinger om Oversættelse 6),
Center for Oversættelse, Engelsk Institut, University of Copenhagen

Herbst, Thomas. 1995
People do not talk in sentences: Dubbing and the idiom principle
In: Gambier (ed.) 1995, 257-271

House, Juliane. 1981
A Model for Translation Quality Assessment.
Gunter Narr Verlag, Tübingen

Ivarsson, Jan & Mary Carroll. 1998.
Subtitling. TransEdit, Simrishamn

Jakobson, Roman. 1966
On Linguistic Aspects of Translation.
In: Reuben Brower (ed.) *On Translation.* 232-239. Oxford University Press, New York.

Jørgensen, Tom Bernbom. 1992
Målgruppeorienteret tv-tekstning.
In: *Tv-tekster: Oversættelse efter mål,* 100-124 (Danske Afhandlinger om Oversættelse 3)
Center for Oversættelse, Engelsk Institut, University of Copenhagen

Kaufmann, Francine. 1998
Aspects de la traduction audiovisuelle en Israël.
In: *Meta,* vol. 43, no. 1, 130-141. Montréal

Karamitroglou, Fotios. 1999
Audiovisual Translation at the Dawn of the Digital Age: Prospects and Potentials
In: *Translation Journal* vol. 3: 3, July 1999: http://accurapid.com/jour-

nal/09av.htm

La Trecchia, Patrizia. 1998
Dubbing: an Italian case study
In: *Perspectives. Studies in Translatology* 1: 1998, 113-124.

Lindberg, Ib (with footnotes by Niels Søndergaard). 1997 to date
Nogle regler om tv-tekstning. www.titlevision.dk/tekstnin.htm

Luyken, G.-M. & T. Herbst; J. Langham-Brown; H. Reid; H. Spinhof. 1991
Overcoming Language Barriers in Television. Dubbing and Subtitling for the European Audience. European Institute for the Media, Manchester (now Düsseldorf)

Marleau, Lucien. 1982
Les sous-titres... Un mal nécessaire
In: *Meta,* vol. 27, no. 3, 271-285. Montréal

Minchinton, John. 1987
Fitting Titles: The Subtitler's Art and the Threat of Euro Titles
In: *Sight & Sound* vol. 56, no. 4, Autumn 1987, 279-282

Papadakis, Iannis. 1998
Greece, a subtitling country
In: Yves Gambier (ed.) *Translating for the Media,* 65-70.
Centre for Translation and Interpreting, University of Turku

Pedersen, Viggo Hjørnager. 1999 (first edition 1997)
Translation Studies Past and Present
In: Henrik Gottlieb (ed.) *An Introduction to Translation Studies*, 47-68.
Center for Translation Studies, English Department, University of Copenhagen

Pedersen Herbener, Jens André & Rune Engelbreth Larsen. 1996a
Bibelforfalskning?
In: *Faklen* no. 1, September 1996, 32-40

Pedersen Herbener, Jens André & Rune Engelbreth Larsen. 1996b
Bibelselskabets retræte & En ny, videnskabelig oversættelse
In: *Faklen* no. 2: November 1996, 33-37 & 40-41

Quargnolo, Mario. 1986
La parola ripudiata. L'incredibile storia dei film stranieri in Italia nei primi anni del sonoro
La cineteca del Friuli, Gemona

Skaarup, Henning. 1981
Da TV var ungt (feature article)
In: *Berlingske Tidende,* August 27. 1981. Copenhagen

Tomaszkiewicz, Teresa. 1993
Les opérations linguistiques qui sous-tendent le processus de sous-titrage des films
Adam Mickiewicz University Press, Poznan.

Toury, Gideon. 1995
Descriptive Translation Studies and beyond
John Benjamins Publishing Company, Amsterdam / Philadelphia

Subtitling in Greece.
The Fear of the Goalie at the Penalty Kick

by
Iannis Papadakis

Since my paper concerns subtitles and cinema, I wanted to subtitle it with a film title. Digging deep in the cinematographic archives of my memory the first film I encountered was the 1962 film by Tony Richardson, *The loneliness of the long distance runner*. Fascinating title, but the revolting character would not help me compare the film with the meticulously programmed and team work that demands the simultaneous subtitling of a film festival. The second title I encountered was *The fear of the Goalie at the Penalty Kick*. Here is my favorite Wim Wenders who, by lending me his film's title, is helping me to explain the process of subtitling simultaneously a film festival. As the projection of the film was going on in the screen of my mind, I was finding common things, but differences too, between a football match and the simultaneous subtitling of a film. Among the common things, we could firstly state the duration. A match lasts 90 minutes, almost as a common length feature film. In Greece, we still have intermissions between the first and the second part, like in football. In some cases it might be longer and last as much as a Manoel de Oliveira film, another one of my favorite directors, giving us annoying and exciting moments with the unexpected hiding behind the next moment. Sports fans want action but no fouls nor penalties against their team. They want the handoffs inside their team. In other words, they seek satisfaction. The cinema-goer is no different. He wants proper subtitles, subtitles with style and personality, subtitles that communicate all the information, do not hide, censor or distort the meaning, subtitles obedient to the subtitler, nice-looking and so discreet that can be invisible.

For all that to take place, the players-subtitlers should be well trained, they should love their game-translation and be willing to give their best, collaborating with the coach-editor and be continuously backed by the sports doctor-programmer. The stadium-cinema should be in excellent condition. Of course there is a difference in scale, and here we have our first major difference between a football match and a simultaneous subtitling. Unlike in a match, where the whole team is responsible for the final result, in the theater only one person takes the responsibility to present to the public the work of a whole team. And that is the subtitler. He alone will be charged for the final result. It all depends on the hand-offs the translator gives him. If they are well timed, the projection goes smoothly. If not… he receives lots of penalties, the audience is unhappy, and he becomes a wretch. The subtitler must play simultaneously the roles of all the players. He must be very watchful. The subtitles must be very obedient children. They should come and go as he commands. Discipline is a must. And if the goalkeeper fears the penalty kick in any game, imagine how he feels in a mundial, or the subtitler in an official première with the presence of the film director.

And if the omnipresent ball is the soul of the game, in simultaneous subtitling we have the total absence of TIME CODE, this fine surgeon's tool that helps us do a perfect job. Unlike film projectors, which run at 24 frames per second, video players run at 25 frames, having thus a frame more. And this one frame spoils the recipe. The film is translated from videotape and is being projected in the theatre with one frame less. And since we can tolerate more easily a bad translation with proper timing, than a good translation with bad timing, the automatic cueing, based on video is excluded from the start. All has to be manual and simultaneous. Any foul is irreversible since there is no referee.

In the recent International Federation of Film Archives Congress in Madrid April 1999, the majority of the directors of the cinemateques worldwide agreed that the manual subtitling is the only solution for the time being. And that, in case of non subtitle-dedicated film copies. And since we mentioned dedicated film copies, we should say that we are not referring to the three major festivals Festival de Cannes, Mostra di Venezia and Berlin Filmspiele, who have the authority and the means to show subtitle-dedicated film copies. And these very copies born during those festivals make then their life throughout the world and arrive to us.

A film to be widely distributed should make itself understood in English, since English, according to Nicolas Negreponte[1], even if it is not the most widely spoken language in the world, it is definitely the most-used second language. It is a utilitarian language that lands planes safely, keeps the Net's infrastructure running and I would personally add make films accessible to non-English speaking countries. Dr. Gottlieb mentioned to me that the films in the Baltic Film Festival are either screened non-subtitled or subtitled only in English.

Some years ago, a new term came to life, "localization", but we tend to forget that the first localized mass-product was the silent movie. The advent of voice recording brought the separation between dubbing and subtitling countries, due mainly to political and nationalistic reason, (Franco in Spain, Mussolini and the Nazis in Italy and in Germany, all wanted to preserve their national identity dubbing all the films in their language, so they could change whatever they didn't like in the scenario). France still does not import films dubbed in French, but not in France. Thus, a film dubbed in French in Canada, cannot be distributed in France, but it can in Belgium. Italo Calvino, in his *Cinema Goer's Autobiography* says: "I sensed that French cinema was talking about things that were disturbing and somehow forbidden, I knew that Jean Gabin in *Quai des Brumes* was not, as the Italian dubbing would have had us believe, a demobbed soldier who wanted to go and work a plantation of colonies, but a deserter escaping from the front, something Fascist censorship would never have allowed a film to discuss."

A last thing I would like to add about dubbing is a new and strange phenomenon that takes place in Greece since last year. Although we belong to the subtitling countries, the efforts of one TV station to mutate us into a dubbing country. They show four to five hours "dubbed" program a day with the worst ever-possible quality. And that's not all. The other two major TV stations are following quite close.

Returning to simultaneous subtitling, and unlike a football match where the ball is omnipresent, we have the omni absence of TIMECODE, the surgeon's tool to cut sharply and precisely the subtitles. So we have

---

[1] Wired, March 1996, p. 112.

to find tricks to simulate as if it were present.

The main problems we have when translating and then subtitling simultaneously a film for a one-time screening are:

- Translation from a non post-production script in English or French and projection of the film with different editing and thus more or less scenes.
- Translation from a pivot language (mainly English) of a film in a third language and projection of the movie with different English subtitles.
- Translation from an English dialogue list of a film in a third language and projection of the film with French subtitles.
- Translation from an English dialogue list of a film in a third language and projection of the film with no subtitles.
- Translation from the original script (English, French, Portuguese, Spanish, German) and projection of the film with English or French subtitles.

A film festival is very demanding. Some 100-200 films shown during 10 days and some 200-400 screenings. That makes about 30-50 projections per day. 10-15 translators can handle all the translations. The simultaneous subtitling is more demanding. It is almost impossible to coordinate the screening so that the translator will also be subtitling the films he has translated. It is commonplace that the subtitler subtitles a film translated by someone else and that, prima-vista, which means that he is seeing it for the first time at the screening for the public. As you can imagine, the unexpected is in the agenda and we have to find means and make the tools to overcome the fouls.

The first subtitling system comprised a fixed display positioned under the theater screen with yellow or red small leads connected to a computer. The subtitles were then shown on that display. But technology made it obsolete and helped us make the system a new and better system. All equipment has to be light and flexible. We need only a video projector and a notebook computer, both fitting in an airplane's carry on compartment. No character generator is needed.

In my experience as a subtitler, and dealing with subtitling software, I found that many of them, the ones at least that are used in Greece, leave a lot to desire. They are made by programmers who do not ask advice from subtitlers and thus make our life miserable. They need a character generator, one more item to carry on. The translators need the basic features of a word processor, a visual image of the subtitle as it is going to be projected and two keys for IN and OUT cues for the simultaneous subtitling.

That's why we made a program from scratch, having in mind that "less is more". So, apart from the editor that displays numbered subtitles boxes, and has FIND, REPLACE, COPY AND PASTE FUNCTIONS, and an orthographic speller, we designed a projection suite that enables the subtitler to have full control over his subtitles, having always in mind that he may subtitle the film prima vista. Which means: his computer screen displays the current subtitle projected and the ten following ones. During the projection he can read quickly the next subtitles and have an idea of what people are going to say in the next one or two minutes so he can be prepared if he has less or more subtitles than what the characters say. Same thing happens if he discovers that he has an extra scene translated, which the director decided not to include at the final editing, but no one thought or cared to inform the translator. So sometimes, he has to jump from 10 to 50 subtitles and find the appropriate one. But until he finds it, the action continues in the film, dialogue is going on and the audience starts to feel uncomfortable and make noise. More loud the noise, less easy he can do his job. Here comes the responsibility of the subtitling responsible who has to hire professional translators to do the job. Unfortunately, this is not always the case. Many inexperienced people translate films in the festivals and make the subtitler's life miserable. His anxiousness may destroy the play.

In order to overcome all the problems that may arise, we tried to find means and tricks to make subtitling go smoothly.

The screen is divided into two columns, one containing the original subtitles and the other the translated. Sometimes, as I enumerated in the problems above, he might have to deal with three languages simultaneously. A Spanish film translated from English, (he has English subtitles in his left column), projected with French subtitles and subtitled finally in Greek. Does he have to be polyglot?

To overcome this very serious and common problem if the film copy has a different editing, we have found a solution. We presubtitle the tape in our studio, transfer it onto a CD-ROM, and play it in the little window we have incorporated in the program, during the projection with some frames ahead. Thus, he knows beforehand what the following scene should be. If it's not what he expected, trouble begins. But fast-forwarding the CD-ROM can lead him quicker to the desired scene and fewer subtitles are lost.He makes less fouls than if he didn't have the support of the subtitled CD-ROM.

When I am explaining the simultaneous subtitling process, people ask me if I am doing the translation simultaneously. They see a person "in the edge of a nervous breakdown" behind his computer screen and cannot understand his feelings. Here is another film title we can borrow from Pedro Almodóvar for our subtitle: "A Subtitler at the edge of a nervous breakdown". You may subtitle a difficult film and almost not follow the action.

Film archives do need a permanent subtitling system, and we have designed our system to satisfy these needs too. In fact, film archives give the translator an exact copy of the film to be projected, so the subtitler can be the G.H. Wells' "Invisible Man". But he needs no bandages. He can be in a separate room and have in his screen instead of the image of the CD-ROM, the image of the theater screen through a camera. In this case, there are no unexpected alterations. New Film Archives Theaters are designed to have a separate room for the subtitler, and in some, he can use the interpreter's booth.

I think it's time the cinema Industry understands they have to care more about subtitle translators. As professor Gambier says, "screen translators are top-level experts with an enormous (social) responsibility, from their intervention in the international (multilingual) exchanges. And since, according to Professor Gottlieb,...the subtitler must possess the musical ears of an interpreter, the stylistic sensitivity of a literary translator, the visual acuteness of a film cutter, and the esthetic sense of a book designer... I think we should be more taken care of.

From the production companies, to prepare post-production scripts, to the responsibles of the festivals who should ask all the material in time. Many times we have to translate only from a dialogue list without any visual support. It is number one in Jan Ivarsson's Code of Good Subtitling Practice: *Subtitlers must always work with a (video, DVD, etc.)*

copy of the production, a copy of the dialogue list and a glossary of unusual words and special references. Alas!

So, how can I distinguish if the one word subtitle "Fire!" is a verb, or a noun? Does he has to fire, to shoot, or is there something that took fire? How can I distinguish genders, sex, plural and singular from an English dialogue list without visual support? I can't.

Another thing we should mention here, is the transformation that is taking place in the subtitling process with the DVD translation. I think this is how we are going to work in the not so far future. Up to now, subtitling was in the care of distribution. So every TV station that shows a film translates it from scratch. DVD is a final product, including the subtitles. The subtitling starts now to be included in the production cost. We don't know what the cinema support will be in the future, but technology enables the studios to include the subtitling with the product they are selling. And since films and DVDs will be released shortly with weeks of difference, they can use the same subtitling, also because DVD is screen and not video subtitling.

Short Description of the CD-ROM "Filoglossia"

by
Frieda Charalabopoulou

"Filoglossia" is a programme for learning Greek as a foreign language and is addressed to absolute or false beginners. It offers supporting material in six languages - English, French, Danish, German, Spanish and Russian.

The programme is based on the communicative approach and focuses on the production and comprehension of both oral and written speech. The user is encouraged to use Greek in order to acquire communicative efficiency and be able to communicate in everyday life situations (e.g. at the airport, at the taverna, at the hotel, at the market, etc).

Each chapter is accompanied by a number of various excercises aiming at the development of all language skills (oral and written speech comprehension, pronunciation exercises, spelling, grammar, formation of sentences, etc), while a number of language tools enables the user to record his/her voice and compare it with a native speaker, to listen to the pronunciation of any Greek word, to look up any word appearing in the programme in the bilingual electronic dictionaries incorporated.

Apart from the language material, the programme also includes rich audio-visual material in order to familiarise the user with the Greek social and cultural situation.

"Filoglossia" was designed and developed by ILSP (Institute for Language and Speech Processing) within the framework of the General Secretariat for Research and Technology project "DIALOGOS".

The main features of the programme are:

- Video and audio files with native speakers
- Familiarisation with the Greek alphabet

- Reading and listening comprehension exercises
- Vocabulary exercises
- Pronunciation exercises with recording facilities
- Spelling exercises
- Grammar exercises
- Voice recognition exercises
- Automatic phonetic transcription of any Greek word
- Use of synthetic voice for the pronunciation of any Greek word
- Bilingual electronic dictionaries
- A tour of the Greek islands (Cyclades)
- Contemporary Greek paintings.

List of Contributors

Lene Andersen
lic. phil. in class. phil.
Vicar
Copenhagen

Frida Charalabopoulou
Institute of Language and
Speech Processing Athens

Otto Steen Due
Department of Greek and Latin
University of Aarhus

Vibeke Espholm
The Nordic Library at Athens

Henrik Gottlieb
Department of English
University of Copenhagen

Rolf Hesse
Translator and lecturer
Gymnasium of Roskilde and
University of Lund

Henrik Holmboe
Aarhus Business School

Niels Jaeger
Translator
Comité des régions, EU
Bruxelles

Takis Kagialis
Director
Center for the Greek Language
Thessaloniki

Leo Kalovyrnas
Translator, BA
Athens

Jørgen Mejer
Director
The Danish Istitute at Athens

Lars Nørgaard
Department of East European Studies
University of Copenhagen

Ioannis Papadakis
Translator
Athens

Aristea Papanikolaou-Christensen
Mag. art. in class. archaeology
Athens and Copenhagen

Dimitrios Napol. Papanikolaou, dr. jur.
Attorney-at-law
Athens

Sophia Scopetea
Translator and lecturer
Department of East European Studies
University of Copenhagen

Minna Skafte Jensen
Department of Greek and Roman Studies
University of Southern Denmark Odense

Christian Gorm Tortzen
Gymnasium of Elsinore and
University of Copenhagen